PENGUIN CLASSICS

CHRONICLE OF THE NARVÁEZ EXPEDITION

ALVAR NÚÑEZ CABEZA DE VACA was born sometime between 1488 and 1492 in the south of Spain, most likely in Jerez de la Frontera. His maternal grandfather, Pedro de Vera, was the well-known conqueror of the Canary Islands. The fourth son of a prominent family, Cabeza de Vaca served as a soldier with the forces of King Carlos V in Italy and later with the Dukes of Medina Sidonia in Spain. Cabeza de Vaca made two trips to the Indies. In 1527, he sailed with Pánfilo de Narváez through Cuba to La Florida, a disastrous expedition whose events he later transformed into the *Chronicle of the Narváez Expedition*, published in 1542. In 1541, he returned to the New World as the governor of the Río de la Plata region in South America, which ended with the mutiny of several of his lieutenants and his being sent back under arrest to Spain, where he was tried for his "crimes," which seem to have been little more than attempts to establish just government for both the Amerindians and the Spanish. These experiences formed the basis for his memoir *Comentarios Reales (Royals Commentaries)*, which was published in 1555 in tandem with the second edition of the *Chronicle of the Narváez Expedition*, and which helped restore his reputation at court. He is believed to have died in about 1560, and was buried near his grandfather in Jerez.

ILAN STAVANS is Lewis-Sebring Professor in Latin American and Latino Culture at Amherst College. His books include *The Hispanic Condition* (1995), *Art and Anger* (1996), *The Oxford Book of Latin American Essays* (1997), *The Riddle of Cantinflas* (1998), *Mutual Impressions* (1999), and *On Borrowed Words* (2001). His work has been translated into six languages.

FANNY BANDELIER was a research anthropologist and teacher who specialized in the cultural history of South America and southwestern North America. She was born Fanny Ritter in 1869 in Zurich, Switzerland, and moved to Lima, Peru, in 1884. There, in 1892, she married Adolph Francis Alphonse Bandelier, an eminent researcher of the pre-Columbian and Hispanic periods of the Americas.

Working together they compiled an impressive body of research findings, until his death in 1914. After his death she held various research and teaching positions, until her death in 1936. Her papers are on deposit in the Adolph Bandelier Collection of the Museum of New Mexico in Santa Fe.

HAROLD AUGENBRAUM is director of The Mercantile Library of New York and its Center for World Literature. Among his recent books are *Growing Up Latino* (1993), *The Latino Reader: An American Literary Tradition from 1542 to the Present* (1997), and *U.S. Latino Literature: A Critical Guide for Students and Teachers* (2000).

ALVAR NÚÑEZ CABEZA DE VACA

Chronicle of the Narváez Expedition

Translated by FANNY BANDELIER
Revised and Annotated by HAROLD AUGENBRAUM
Introduction by ILAN STAVANS

PENGUIN BOOKS

PENGUIN BOOKS
Published by the Penguin Group
Penguin Group (USA) Inc., 375 Hudson Street, New York, New York 10014, U.S.A.
Penguin Group (Canada), 90 Eglinton Avenue East, Suite 700, Toronto, Ontario,
Canada M4P 2Y3 (a division of Pearson Penguin Canada Inc.)
Penguin Books Ltd, 80 Strand, London WC2R 0RL, England
Penguin Ireland, 25 St Stephen's Green, Dublin 2, Ireland
(a division of Penguin Books Ltd)
Penguin Group (Australia), 250 Camberwell Road, Camberwell, Victoria 3124,
Australia (a division of Pearson Australia Group Pty Ltd)
Penguin Books India Pvt Ltd, 11 Community Centre, Panchsheel Park,
New Delhi – 110 017, India
Penguin Group (NZ), 67 Apollo Drive, Rosedale, North Shore 0632, New Zealand
(a division of Pearson New Zealand Ltd)
Penguin Books (South Africa) (Pty) Ltd, 24 Sturdee Avenue, Rosebank,
Johannesburg 2196, South Africa

Penguin Books Ltd, Registered Offices: 80 Strand, London WC2R 0RL, England

*The Journey of Alvar Núñez Cabeza de Vaca and his Companions from
Florida to the Pacific, 1528–1536,* translated by Fanny Bandelier, published in
the United States of America by A.S. Barnes & Company, 1905
This edition with a new introduction and revised translation
published in Penguin Books 2002

9   10

Introduction copyright © Ilan Stavans, 2002
Revised translation and notes copyright © Harold Augenbraum, 2002
All rights reserved

LIBRARY OF CONGRESS CATALOGING IN PUBLICATION DATA
Núñez Cabeza de Vaca, Alvar, 16th cent.
[Relación y comentarios. English]
Chronicle of the Narváez expedition / Alvar Núñez Cabeza de Vaca ;
translated by Fanny Bandelier ; revised and annotated by Harold Augenbratum ;
introduction by Ilan Stavans.
p. cm.—(Penguin classics)
Includes bibliographical references.
ISBN 978-0-14-243707-0 (pbk.)
1. Núñez Cabeza de Vaca, Alvar, 16th cent. 2. Narváez, Pánfilo de, d. 1528.
3. America—Discovery and exploration—Spanish. 4. America—Description
and travel. 5. America—Early accounts to 1600. 6. Indians of North America
—History—16th century. 7. Explorers—America—Biography. 8. Explorers—
Spain—Biography. I. Augenbraum, Harold. II. Title. III. Series.
E125.N9 A3 2002
973.1'6—dc21   2001058315

Printed in the United States of America
Set in Stempel Garamond

CONTENTS

CONTENTS

INTRODUCTION

We Americans are yet to really learn our own antecedents. . . . Thus far, impress'd by New England writers and schoolmasters, we tacitly abandon ourselves to the notion that our United States have been fashion'd from the British Islands only . . . which is a very great mistake.

—Walt Whitman, 1883

Desnudo . . . In Spanish the word means "naked," and it's the way Alvar Núñez Cabeza de Vaca likes to describe himself in his *Chronicle of the Narváez Expedition*. In straightforward fashion, the chronicle narrates his trekking between 1527 and 1536, from Cuba to Florida and Texas, onward to New Mexico and Arizona, and down to Mexico. "I wandered through many very strange lands, lost and naked," he claims at one point, and then, at another, "This is the only thing that a man who left there naked could bring back with him." This is, no doubt, a surprising, even perplexing, way to describe the state of an Iberian conquistador in his colonial quest across the American continent. Readers from the sixteenth century to the present have gotten used to adventures of courage and domination from the likes of Pizarro and Hernán Cortés. Adjectives like *gallant, intrepid, assertive,* and *outlandish* easily come to mind. But not *naked*, which stands as an attribute of vulnerability and misfortune—not part of the mythical image of valor the machinery of the Spanish Empire spread throughout the New World from 1523 to the period of independence around 1810.

Then again, Cabeza de Vaca isn't your typical vanquisher. The self-portrait that emerges of him and his three close companions in *La relación*, as the chronicle is commonly known in Spanish (the other favorite title is *Naufragios*) and in some English renditions as "The Account," is one colored by stupefaction. A veritable descent into chaos—that is the way I prefer to see it. The *Chronicle of the Narváez Expedition* should be read, I'm convinced, as a Dantean pilgrimage through the chambers of hell and purgatory. In modern times, this type of literature is made famous by books like Joseph Conrad's *Heart of Darkness*, in which the European traveler finds himself, unexpectedly, at the edge of the earth, alone and lonely and unsure of his culture. It is a journey that gives room to a process of reinvention: a member of a noble lineage, Cabeza de Vaca becomes a doctor (not by accident and a hint of irony has he been called "the first surgeon of Texas"), a shaman, and a hero to the natives.

In his version of his adventure, Cabeza de Vaca is perhaps more honest and less falsifying than many of his contemporaries. After all, the myth of the conquistador as a mighty, larger-than-life *macho* has been under fire almost from the moment the Iberian army arrived on American shores. Friar Bartolomé de Las Casas, the so-called "defender of the Indians" and the main source of dissemination of this Black Legend, accused his fellow countrymen of cruel, merciless acts of violence and sexual excess against the Indian population in the New World. He was one, although certainly the most prominent, among a handful of early witnesses and participants in the endeavor of colonization that acted as a voice of conscience. But, in truth, their reproach didn't get them too far, not far enough at least. It is no secret that the Americas, unexplored—i.e., magical—as they were, were perceived in Spain and elsewhere on the Old Continent as a virginal landscape, a place for experimentation. Beyond the direct supervision of the crown Iberian testosterone went on a rampage.

To this day apologists refuse to acknowledge the destructive impulses nurtured by the conquistadors and, instead, justify the effort by any means possible. One of them is the eponymous Oxford scholar Salvador de Madariaga, author of biographies of Christopher Columbus and the nineteenth-century *libertador* Simón Bolívar. In his book *The Rise of the Spanish Empire* (1947), Madariaga argues:

> The men who explored and conquered America did so with the scantiest material means. Their spirit did it all. Colón had set the example discovering the New World with the three caravels, the biggest

of which was 140 tons. Cabeza de Vaca walked through thousands of miles of unexplored country in both the northern and the southern parts of the continent. Cortés conquered Mexico with four hundred men and sixteen horses. Official help was seldom given, in fact seldom asked for, by these men who preferred to go ahead without shackles. They nearly always applied for some official sanction before starting on their expeditions of exploration and conquest, but what they sought at court was less money, weapons, ships, and horses, than the moral force to legitimate authority. No man will ever understand the Conquest who does not give its due value to this feature of it: spirited, undisciplined, anarchical, the conquerors are nevertheless obsessed by the majesty of the law and not only do they never . . . stand up against the king of Spain, who, distant and enigmatic, follows their fabulous adventures with an eye worried and distracted by Luther-ridden Europe, but they actually seek the sanction of the royal word for their deeds and status.

Why? Because these Spaniards were all imbued with the sense of common fellowship fostered in Spain as in all the Latin world by the twofold tradition of Rome—the Imperial and the Christian. They were, in one world, deeply *civilized*. Many of them behaved damnably. The extermination of the natives of the islands was in part at least due to the outburst of violence which followed the first discoveries and conquests. But this very outburst of disorder and anarchy which took place in the first years was but the explosion of energies restrained by civilized standards, on finding themselves suddenly liberated on the edge of the world of authority.

Despite this pronouncement, not all stories of the conquistadors fit Madariaga's mold. The story of Alvar Núñez Cabeza de Vaca rather becomes an object lesson in the history of the conquest of America. He failed, but turned failure into success. He lost, and then regained, his sense of *la civilización*. In our reading from the perspective of the twenty-first century, he tells a tale of imposture and transformation, leading to a reexamination of our own ideas about cultural interaction.

Who was Alvar Núñez Cabeza de Vaca? What were his actual accomplishments as an explorer? What type of response did the *Chronicle of the Narváez Expedition* generate among his contemporaries and future readers? Was he accurate in his descriptions? What role did memory—persona and collective—play in the composition of it? How did his life evolve once he became known as an explorer of the northern regions of the American continent? And what is his status in history?

For a long time, the biographical information available on him was despairingly limited. Cabeza de Vaca—in Spanish, the patronymic literally means *Cow's Head*—is one of the stranger surnames in literary and cultural history. It is believed to have developed from the following legend, probably apocryphal, disseminated by one of the explorer's nineteenth-century translators, Thomas Buckingham Smith. In 1212, in the battle between Moors and Christians of Las Navas de Tolosa in northern Spain, a shepherd by the name of Martín Alhaja used a cow's skull to mark an open path through which the Christian army, surrounded by its enemy, not only escaped but also managed to win the battle. In recognition, the Spanish king gave the shepherd the official title of *Cabeza de Vaca*. The story cannot be proved, however, since the family name does not appear in administrative or court records until centuries later.

The explorer's more immediate ancestry had distinguished lineage and roots in Jerez de la Frontera and Zamora in southern and western Spain. In the concluding chapter of his chronicle to Florida, the author states that he is "Alvar Nuñez Cabeza de Vaca, son of Francisco de Vera and grandson of Pedro de Vera, who conquered the Canary Islands. His mother was called Doña Teresa Cabeza de Vaca, and she was a native of Xerez de la Frontera." The mention of his grandfather, Pedro de Vera, was significant. He was famous for the conquest of the largest of the Canary Islands, the Gran Canaria, and, even though he apparently died poor, such financial straits didn't prevent him from obtaining the honor of burial in the Dominican monastery of Santo Domingo el Real in Jerez de la Frontera. Unquestionably, the genealogical tree inspired the future *conquistador,* whose dream it was—to the extent that the reference to his parents and military grandfather in *La relación* is any indication—to follow in the footsteps of his forebears.

It is believed that Cabeza de Vaca was born between 1485 and 1492, dates derived from the study of a collection of legal documents, such as trusteeship (*curatela*), petitions, and letters of donation. This seven-year period was of utmost importance in Spanish history, an era of expansion abroad and intense political and social reconfiguration at home, as well as intellectual enlightenment. It coincided with the end of the *Reconquista*, the reconquest of the Iberian peninsula from the Islamic Moors by the Catholic royalty, Ferdinand and Isabella, who hoped both to reclaim the peninsula from the Moors and to turn Christianity into the peninsula's unifying religion. It included Columbus's first voyage across the Atlantic Ocean and the expulsion of the Jews as well as the publication of the first grammar of the Spanish language, by Antonio de Nebrija. Great changes were occurring, and the collective spirit of exhilaration surely left its mark on the country's youth, including Alvar Núñez Cabeza de Vaca.

The details of Cabeza de Vaca's early life are scanty. Roughly between 1502 and 1527, he worked for a series of dukes of Medina Sidonia, one of the oldest Spanish ducal houses to be formed by the king. (Other members of the Cabeza de Vaca family also lived at the duke's court.) He was one of the duke's stewards (*camarero*), a personal attendant. As such, according to an anecdote promoted by scholar Juan Francisco Maura, he was witness to the marital impotence between the duke Alonso de Guzmán and the duchess Ana de Aragón, in which the duke's sexual behavior was questioned. The witness's account was given in 1532, however, when Cabeza de Vaca was in Texas. Apparently he had given those accounts to a cousin of his, who in turn offered them in the case brought between the married parties. To prove the duke's impotence, according to the story, he and another employee brought to the duke's chamber "two or three women who attempted but failed to arouse him." In his 1998 Spanish edition of *Naufragios*, Maura dwelled on this anecdote, the importance of which, at far as the explorer's biography goes, is to allow the reader a sense of the social codes of the time and the voyeuristic role Cabeza de Vaca had in the estate of his employer.

Cabeza de Vaca's military career included participation in the company that traveled to Italy to take Naples. Apparently he also took part in the 1512 attack on Bologna and the fortress of the duke of Ferrara. The goal was to help Pope Julius II, whose forces were under attack by the French. Sources state that in the same year Cabeza de Vaca also fought in the decisive battle of Ravenna, in which the Spaniards were ultimately defeated by the French. He also participated in the effort in 1520 by the Duque de Medina Sidonia to put down a *Comunero* revolt in Seville, a popular uprising against converted Jews known as *conversos*, and was supported by another ducal house, that of Arcos, an Andalucian heredity. Probably around the same time he married María Marmolejo, who, some scholars believe, came from a *converso* family. Between then and his decision to join the Narváez expedition to Florida, little is known of his whereabouts or activities.

Juan Ponce de León had "discovered" the territory of Florida in 1513 and named it for the time of year in which he landed, Easter Day, *Pascua Florida*. He stayed only a short period of time. He found the terrain to be inhospitable and its inhabitants unfriendly, so he returned to Puerto Rico. It is likely that between then and the arrival of Narváez's fleet, other Spaniards visited the region, most likely to capture slaves. Sources establish that in the early part of the sixteenth century Pánfilo de Narváez (1480?–1528) had lived in Cuba and Hispañola, the latter known today as Haiti and the Dominican Republic, and that he took part in Juan de Esquivel's 1509 conquest of Jamaica. Sometime between 1520 and 1524 he was imprisoned in Veracruz by Hernán Cortés, who suspected that he was intriguing for power in Mexico. He returned to Spain after his release. By virtue of his previous experience in the Indies—and, perhaps too, as a result of his intrigues in the Spanish court and in the New World—Narváez was awarded the governorship (*Adelantado*) of the southeastern part of North America, *La Florida*.

The Narváez expedition embarked from Spain with five ships and a crew of about six hundred men, which included at least two accompanying Catholic priests. They sailed out of Sanlúcar de Barrameda, a Mediterranean port at the mouth of the Guadalquivir River, stopped briefly in the Canary Islands, in mid-August arrived in Hispañola, and then continued to Cuba. Almost from the start, the journey was doomed. On Cuba, they encountered a hurricane and lost two ships and scores of men. After crossing to the mainland, they found the inhabitants hostile and the availability of food low. At some point they made the fateful decision to abandon their ships and three quarters of the expeditionary force marched inland. About three hundred men died on this trek and its aftermath in small boats, and the four survivors—the Moroccan slave, Estebanico, Andrés Dorantes, Alonso del Castillo Maldonado, and Cabeza de Vaca himself—began a journey along the approximate inland route that, in today's topographical coordinates, started near Austin and San Antonio, went northward toward the Colorado

River, and then on to the region of Midland, Pecos, Carlsbad, the region of El Paso, and finally south to Culiacán, Guadalajara, and Mexico City in present-day Mexico. Soon after Cabeza de Vaca and his three companions reached Mexico City, he cowrote with Dorantes and Maldonado an account of the expedition known as the *Joint Report*, which has been lost, and in the spring of 1537 he returned to Spain.

Cabeza de Vaca spent the years between 1537 and 1540 in Spain seeking a royal commission and preparing his chronicle. His dream was to become *Adelantado* of Florida. The historian Sancho de Sopranis uncovered a document that makes it clear that the explorer asked the king to name him to that post, but instead gave it to Hernando de Soto, whose own experience in the southeastern United States would also become an object lesson in failure. So the author of *La relación* focused his energy on procuring a similar position in the Río de la Plata, in the region known today as Argentina and Paraguay, after the death by starvation of the person who had held the job, Pedro de Mendoza. In 1540, by royal contract, Cabeza de Vaca became governor of the province of La Plata and also *Adelantado* of any new lands that might be discovered. There is no question that he was both a witness and a participant in times of rapid change. The age of Spanish exploration was quickly coming to an end in the New World, replaced by a move to institutionalize the viceroyship of the various lands conquered in these efforts. "Just as he and his fellows returning to New Spain [i.e., Mexico] from the wilderness of Florida in 1537 had to come to grips with the end of the period of freewheeling entrepreneurship on the American mainland," argue Rolena Adorno and Charles Pautz in their scholarly edition of the *Chronicle*, "so too his appointment in 1540 to the exalted titles of *Adelantado* and governor came at a time when the power and privilege therein promised were harder than ever to achieve." He held these positions between 1541 and 1545, but his power, if any, quickly eroded. The title of *Adelantado* usually generated animosity—this was the case of Narváez and such other governors as Diego Velázquez, Vasco Núñez de Balboa, Mendoza, and others. Indeed, those under Cabeza de Vaca's tutelage rebelled against him, and he was eventually arrested and brought back to Spain in chains.

Back in the Iberian Peninsula in 1546 four different lawsuits were brought against him. These concerned abuse of power and violence against the native population. He started the trial imprisoned, but eventually was moved into house arrest (the period in South America and his return home is chronicled in his second and only other book, *Comentarios*). This was a period of intense suffering for Cabeza de Vaca, mainly as a result of the public embarrassment he suffered. In 1551 a sentence was decreed that stripped him of his titles, banned him from returning to the New World, and sent him to a penal colony in Algeria. He appealed, and the case was reopened, which resulted in a reduction of his sentence the following year. His banishment from American lands was limited to the Río de la Plata, and he was not sent to the penal colony. Still, his titles had been revoked. He petitioned for compensation for lost assets. After some negotiation, some of that compensation took place. In short, he was exonerated. But the injury of an eight-year affront was done. When the 1555 edition of *Relación y comentarios* was released, Cabeza de Vaca was apparently stationed in Seville. Between then and 1559, the probable date of his death, he returned to Jerez de la Frontera. For a while historians assumed that his trial left him poor, and thus, that he died "penniless, old, and broken-hearted," as Morris Bishop claimed in his biography *The Odyssey of Cabeza de Vaca* (1933). But recent scholarship points in a different direction. He was alive and well in the late winter and early spring of 1559, and it is believed he was buried in the same place where his military grandfather was laid, the Real Convento de Santo Domingo. He was known to have paid a ransom for a relative held captive in Algiers, so the reports of his poverty are likely to be exaggerations.

In Cabeza de Vaca's chronicle the protagonists are anything but triumphant. They lose everything: their clothes, tools, horses, compatriots, and even their dignity. They wander about in a strange, unmapped land with no other objective than to get back to the seemingly ordered world of Spanish settlement. In their journey they encounter scores of natural and human obstacles, as well as various previously "undiscovered" Indian tribes, each with its own language and customs. To Cabeza de Vaca and his peers, this serves as an opportunity to test their faith and demeanor. It allows him to "observe." He persuades himself—and attempts to convince the reader—that he is a fine protoanthropologist.

The sense of newness in the environment is patent in his voice at every turn. His intent in drafting the narrative is to impress on his reader—and, especially, on Spain's king, Charles V, to whom it is targeted, at least nominally—the view that the territories in Florida and the Southwest are legitimate for colonization. Upheld by expansionary ideas, at once secular and religious, Spain in the first half of the sixteenth century pursued territories beyond its immediate surroundings. So Cabeza de Vaca struggles, as much as possible, to offer a benign portrait, even if his miseries keep mounting up: the soil is fertile, the Indians are friendly, and the chances of exploration and exploitation are obvious. This is not the same self-promoting naïveté one finds in Columbus's diaries and those of other early voyagers, though. A more stolid, ironlike approach is sensed in Hernán Cortés's *Cartas de relación*. (Beatriz Pastor has an enlightening study about the paradigms of conquest.) Cabeza de Vaca, unlike most others, recognizes himself from early on as a disoriented sightseer. His account has incoherent passages. Worse, the number of inconsistencies in it is startling. For instance, he states at one point in his *Chronicle of the Narváez Expedition*: "In the two thousand leagues we traveled, on land, and by sea in boats, and in the ten months more after our rescue from captivity that we untiringly walked across the land, nowhere did we come upon either sacrifices or idolatry." But elsewhere, he describes pagan religious practices and acts of cannibalism. While he perceives himself as knowledgeable and authoritative, he appears also keenly aware of the plethora of mistreatment and profanation his own people indulge in. So he proclaims that "to bring all these people to Christianity and subjection to Your Imperial Majesty, they must be won by kindness, the only certain way." And he adds:

While we were welcomed everywhere, those who came with us treated those who received us badly, taking away their homes and belongings without leaving them anything. It saddened us to see how those who were so good to us were abused. Besides, we feared that this behavior might cause trouble and strife. But we could not dare to interfere or punish the transgressors, and had to wait until we had more authority over them. Furthermore, the sufferers themselves, when they noticed how badly we felt, consoled us by telling us not to worry; that they were happy to see their homes so well employed, and that, besides, further on they would repay themselves from other Indians, who were very rich.

The image of the undressed explorer, *el viajero desnudo,* is a useful one in that, in *La relación*, Cabeza de Vaca portrays himself as a wanderer "through many very strange lands, lost and naked," and he perceives the Indians as "tall and naked," suggesting that "they were wonderfully built, very thin, strong, and agile." In other words, *naked*, in more than a dozen textual appearances, stands as a double attribute: it signifies bewilderment, even embarrassment on the part of the voyager, and is also used to indicate an uncontaminated, natural disposition toward the environment by the natives. This is a semidemocratic quality that, I suspect, is one of the reasons the narrative has become so popular over the last 150 years: in it, America—simultaneously understood as the continent and, à la Robert Frost, "the nation" before it became such—distills a libertarian zest that erases difference by pushing its inhabitants to the limit.

Cabeza de Vaca offers an excruciating account of his journey, delivering comments on various Indian tribes he encountered and their respective customs, the faith in Jesus Christ that kept him alive, and the flora and fauna that surrounded him. The fact that he survived the tribulation and left a record of it makes him, willy-nilly, the first voyager across the American continent. In his account, Cabeza de Vaca described the internal struggles for power and authority, and then delved into the various calamities— hurricanes, swamps, snakes, and treacherous paths through brutal vegetation—that plagued them. He and Narváez parted ways, and Cabeza de Vaca and his group suffered illness, hunger, and terrible weather. Among the most useful assets of the chronicle is information about the Indian tribes Cabeza de Vaca and his companions came across in their journey. This aspect has attracted anthropologists and literary scholars. Enrique Pupo-Walker, in his English edition of 1993, included an appendix that lists almost a dozen recognizable tribes, from the Apalachees to the Coahuiltecans. If the readers follow the narrative carefully, it becomes clear that Cabeza de Vaca often feels at odds with what he sees, how different it is from his own traditional lifestyle. More often than not, he is humble and nonjudgmental. Chapter 26, in which he lists various groups and languages, is enthralling. "There are two distinct languages spoken on the island," he states, "those of one language are called Cavoques, those of the other Han." He also registers the

Charruco Indians, the Deguenes, the Mendicans, the Quevenes, and so on. He adds: "All of them have houses and villages and speak different languages. Among them there is a language in which when they call men to look at something they say 'arraca' and for dogs they say 'xó.' " Soon after, he describes the use and properties of tobacco, used by them to "get inebriated." The portrayal of rituals is symptomatic of Cabeza de Vaca's overall approach to the natives. He perceives them not as enemies but as friends, although he is constantly on guard and uses demeaning commentaries to describe their behavior. In one of the most controversial sections of the book, chapter 19, he goes as far as to describe the Indian population as, again, *uncivilized*. He announces: "All over the land there are vast and handsome pastures, with good grass for cattle, and it strikes me that the soil would be very fertile were the country inhabited and improved by reasoning people." On the contrary, his descriptions are filled with images of back-stabbing acts, ambushes, and other acts of revenge.

Civilized, uncivilized. . . These are much contested words today. The *Oxford English Dictionary (OED)* finds its semantic roots in *civis*, from the Greek "citizen," then defines it as "a developed or advanced state of human society." In our skeptical age, though, "developed" and "advanced," as categories, are problematic: developed and advanced in comparison to whom? It is by now clear from historical sources that the Aztec and Mayan empires encountered by the Spaniards were no less militaristic but also fully developed in political and intellectual terms. More useful than the *OED* to our discussion is *Tesoro de la Lengua Castellana o Española*, by Sebastián de Covarrubias, a dictionary of the Spanish language published in 1611, some fifty years after Cabeza de Vaca died, which eventually became the urtext in Iberian lexicography. Neither *civilización* nor *América* are defined in it because these two terms didn't become part of regular speech until the second half the eighteenth century, as the movement toward emancipation in the thirteen British colonies took hold and, a bit later, France engaged in a revolution that brought the bourgeoisie to power. Thus, they are absent from Cabeza de Vaca's vocabulary. Covarrubias does include an entry for *ciudad* ("city"), which he defines as a *"multitud de hombres ciudadanos, que se ha consagrado a vivir en un mesmo lugar, debajo de unas leyes y un gobierno"* (a multiplicity of male citizens, consecrated to a life in the same place, under a set of laws and a government). And he also offers a lengthy interpretation of the term *bárbaro*, of which this sentence is an integral part: *"a los que son ignorantes sin letras, a los de malas costumbres y mal morigerados, a los esquivos que no admiten la comunicación de los demás hombres de razón, que viven sin ella, llevados de sus apetitos, y finalmente los que son despiadados y crueles"* (those that are ignoramuses without education, those that have bad customs and have badly engaged with others, those that refuse to admit communication with other men of reason, that live without reason, controlled by their appetites, and, finally, those that are unmerciful and cruel).

Needless to say, these absences and inclusions are symptomatic. Cabeza de Vaca might not use the word *civilización*, but he unequivocally grasps the meaning we have given it today. His is a flamboyant ethnographic eye. His nakedness, in metaphorical terms at least, allows him a privileged standpoint from which to observe and judge what his eyes see. Herein a description of an Indian drink and the ceremony it brings about:

> They also drink something that they extract from leaves of a tree similar to a water-oak, toasting them on the fire in a container like a low-necked bottle. When the leaves are toasted they fill the container with water and hold it over the fire for long enough for the water to boil twice. Then they pour the liquid into a bowl made of a gourd cut in half. When there is a lot of foam on it they drink it as hot as they can stand, and from the time they take it out of the first vessel until they drink they shout, "Who wants to drink?" When women hear this they stand still, and although they may be carrying a very heavy load they do not dare to move. Should one of them stir, she is dishonored and beaten. In a great rage they spill the liquid they have prepared and spit up what they drank, easily and without pain. The reason for this custom, they say, is that when they want to drink that water and the women stir from the spot where they first hear the shouts, an evil substance gets into the liquid that penetrates their bodies, causing them to die before long. All the time the water boils the vessel must be kept covered. Should it be uncovered while a woman comes along they pour it out and do not drink it. It is yellow and they drink it for three days without partaking of any food.

Perhaps a more edgy description, also in chapter 26, is the one in which the chronicler refers to homosexuality. "During the time I was among [the Indian tribes]," he claims, "I saw something very repulsive, namely, a man married to another. These are impotent and womanish beings, who dress like women and do the work of women. They carry heavy loads but do not use a bow. Among these Indians we saw many of them. They are more robust than other men, taller, and can carry heavy loads." And in his *Comentarios* he discusses the way Spaniards used Indian women as concubines. In *La relación*, though, the scattered references by Cabeza de Vaca to women among the natives does add up to a group portrait of sorts. For instance, he argues that among one of the tribes he encountered, "We found the women better treated than in any other part of the Indies as far as we have seen. They wear shirts of cotton that reach as far as the knee, and over them half-sleeves of scraped deerskin, with strips that hang down to the ground, and which they clean with certain roots that clean very well and thus keep them tidy. The shirts are open in front and tied with strings; they wear shoes." More often than not, though, he describes the way male Indians "dishonor and beat" their women, which, for them, he says, is part of a regular domestic behavior. This group portrait, it should be added, is in contrast with the picture of the Spanish women offered, particularly in the end of his chronicle, where he claims to have heard "a woman saying to the other women that, since their husbands had gone inland to place themselves in such imminent danger, they should not think of them any longer, but at once look for other husbands; that she was going to do it, for her part. So she and the others married and lived with those that were on board the vessels."

An especially significant reference for those interested in literary echoes is Cabeza de Vaca's passing comment about a village of blind Indians. This comment was introduced by the chronicler into the 1555 edition in Valladolid. (It appears, in this version, in the notes.) He states in chapter 28 that one day he and his companions arrived at a village. In it some Indians "brought us all the people of [it]; most of them had one eye clouded, while others were totally blind from the same cause, which amazed us. They were well built, of very good physique, and whiter than any we had met until then." This reference, of course, recalls the famous story "The Country of the Blind," by H. G. Wells, as well as one of the seven paradoxical tales by Oliver Sacks in *An Anthropologist on Mars*. And in an important passage regarding interracial relations in the Americas since the sixteenth century, Cabeza de Vaca described what might be taken, with a stretch of understanding, as the birth of the *mestizo*, the mixed race of Spanish and *indio*. This thesis, suggested by Maura and other scholars, focuses on the following statement in *La relación*: "It happened frequently that women of our company would give birth to children and forthwith bring them to have the sign of the cross made over them and the babes be touched by us." The passage, vintage Cabeza de Vaca in its outright ambiguity, might not be sufficient evidence to support the argument, though. Other passages might even refute this thesis; for instance the one about the Spaniards not speaking much to the Indians, sending Estevanico to talk to them instead in order to maintain a distance. Plus, notice he doesn't use the term *mestizo* directly. It was another chronicler of the Spanish colonization, the "El Inca" Garcilaso de la Vega (1539–1616), who used the rubric for the first time, to denote a person of mixed Spanish and Indian heritage. *Mestizaje*, connoted by him, has become an ever-popular, and also controversial racial process, especially in Mexico and Central America, reflected upon, among many others, by José Vasconcelos in *The Cosmic Race* (1927) and Octavio Paz in *The Labyrinth of Solitude* (1950). But even if Cabeza de Vaca is an unlikely originator of the rubric, it is fundamental to point out that in the final chapters of the *Chronicle of the Narváez Expedition*, he undergoes a startling metamorphosis—in his physical appearance, as well as in his sympathy for the Indians. They, in turn, see him as unlike any other Spaniard. Should this not be seen as a beginning to the cultural *mestizaje* in the Americas?

There is a more urgent, polemical issue one needs to address, though: Cabeza de Vaca's accuracy. William T. Pilkington once described him as "not only a physical trailblazer; he was also a literary pioneer, and he deserves the distinction of being called the Southwest's first writer." Pilkington added: "The *Relación*, while not fiction, possesses most of the attributes of a good novel." In fact, I dare to add that it might be better to describe it as such: a fictional account, or perhaps a factual novel, for Cabeza de Vaca has a most unorthodox approach to facts. Either way, its accuracy is put in question, an attitude already prevalent during his own day and age.

Gonzalo Fernández de Oviedo y Valdés (1478–1557) also wrote an account of the Narváez expedition, included in *Historia general y natural de las Indias* (book 35, chapters 1–7), against which Cabeza de Vaca's must be read. Not only has such an account been described as *"el máximo ejemplo de la insensatez e improvisación"* (the supreme example of stupidity and improvisation) by scholars such as Trinidad Barrera, it has also been attacked as untrustworthy since the beginning. These questions should be asked: What was Cabeza de Vaca's objective in *La relación*? Who was his target reader? Did he have a specific agenda in mind when he drafted the manuscript, about half a decade after the events took place? "No service is left to me," he argued in the prologue dedicated to the king, "but to bring an account to Your Majesty of the nine years I wandered. . . . In this way you will know and understand the manner of the lands and the provinces in them, what foods and animals grow there, the customs of the many barbarous nations with which I had contact and lived, and many other details that I was able to experience and know so that in some way I will have been of service to Your Majesty." Service to the king, then, is his aim, and he pretends to be at once truthful and objective. But to what extent is he?

It has been argued, for sure, that the conditions in which he wrote were far from optimal. Either way, the flamboyance of *La relación* has generated much controversy. Some have even dared to compare it to the twentieth-century "magical realist" fiction produced by authors such as Gabriel García Márquez, which includes forgotten generals, clairvoyant prostitutes, and epidemics of insomnia. There are sections in Cabeza de Vaca's narrative with the exact same flavor, such as the one in chapter 38, in which, while Cabeza de Vaca is still on board one of the ships, a woman offers Narváez an omen of the miseries to come. She claims to be passing down the prophecy. As is often the case in these types of tales, the forecaster is frequently a person in the fringes, perhaps ethnically different. This is the case, since the woman patently received the message from an Arab woman from Hornachos, Spain:

> Among them were ten married women, one of whom had foretold the governor many things that afterward happened to him.
> When he marched inland she warned him not to go, saying that neither he nor any of his company would return, and that, should

any come back, God would work miracles through him, since she felt sure that few, or none, would escape. The governor responded that he and all who went with him expected to fight and conquer many very strange people and countries, so that, while many would have to die in the conquest, he was sure, from the accounts he had of the richness of the country, that the survivors would be fortunate and become very wealthy, according to the information about the riches that land contained. He asked the woman to tell him who it was that had acquainted her with the things, past and present, of which she had spoken. She answered that in Castile a Moorish woman from Hornachos had told her what she said to us before we left there, all of which took place as predicted.

Be that as it may, "magic realism" as a category has its origins in the surrealist movement, especially in the attempt by André Breton and others to explore the language of myth and dreams and, also, by their fascination with the virginal, "land-before-time" aspect of nature and folklore in the Americas, as seen from a European perspective. After a trip to Haiti, Alejo Carpentier, the Cuban intellectual, wrote in the prologue to his novel *The Kingdom of This World* (1943) about *"lo real maravilloso,"* a mix of the trivial and the surprising. "I realized," he says, "that the presence and authority of the real marvelous was not a privilege unique to Haiti but the patrimony of all the Americas, where, for example, a census of cosmogonies is still to be established." Cabeza de Vaca's proclivity to invent, to fantasize, is unquestionable. And yet he is not keen to mythologize, nor does he use language to build alternative realities. Still, he is aware that his testimony is the first description of a previously unseen reality, and thus, that he is, like Adam and Eve, a source. This biblical component has prompted some to turn him into a fountainhead of sorts of post–World War II literature. Since it "often undertakes the primal task of naming the unknown," argues Pupo-Walker, "its naming action links Cabeza de Vaca's *Relación* to myth as well as to powerful imaginative writings represented today [. . .] by *One Hundred Years of Solitude* (1967) and Mario Vargas Llosa's *War of the End of the World* (1981)."

Another crucial element in the reader's understanding of the chronicle is Cabeza de Vaca's messianic drive. According to critic Juan Francisco Maura, the word *Dios*, meaning God in Spanish, is *"la más frecuente en toda la narración"* (the most frequent in the whole narration). The statement is an estimate of how deep the chronicler sees his involvement with the Catholic faith. Throughout the narrative, he portrays himself as a prophet, as a shaman with unique powers to heal and comfort the Indians. He talks of how the Indians "came to us so we might touch and make the sign of the cross over them. They were so obtrusive that they made it difficult to endure, since everyone, sick and healthy, wanted to be blessed." And, taking advantage of a pretended ignorance on their part, he adds: "Among all those people it was believed that we came from Heaven. What they do not understand or is new to them they are wont to say it comes from above." He even invokes, in strict personal terms, the passion of Jesus Christ, "our Savior [. . .] and the blood he shed for me," and he considers, "how much greater his sufferings had been from the thorns, than those I was then enduring." Is this, a self-comparison? Thus the religiosity of Cabeza de Vaca is crucial. This element is emphasized in the film *Cabeza de Vaca*, made in 1993 and directed by Nicolás Echevarría, with actors Juan Diego, Daniel Giménez Cacho, and Roberto Sosa. To the best of my knowledge, this is the only theatrical movie ever made with a screenplay adapted from *La relación*. Curiously, it is a coproduction between, among other entities, Mexico's Instituto Mexicano de Cinematografía, Spain's Televisión Española, England's Channel Four Television, and American Playhouse Theatrical Films. This results in a shifting historical viewpoint that neither condemns nor celebrates the colonial enterprise by the Iberian soldiers and explorers on this side of the Atlantic. At any rate, in the film the protagonist is presented as a half-crazed wanderer with prophetic attributes who lives among the Indians portraying himself as a messiah. This, to some extent, is an accurate description. Cabeza de Vaca, in the *Chronicle of the Narváez Expedition*, is a wizard and a fortune-teller, a healer and a prophet. As he persuades the reader, the Indians responded to his claims with naïveté.

The trajectory of Cabeza de Vaca's narrative in its various editions and translations also deserves attention. The first account, called the *Joint Report*, was dictated by Cabeza de Vaca, Dorantes, and Maldonado while they were still in the Americas. It has been lost, but it was used by the historian Fernández de Oviedo in the sixteenth century to develop a history of the Narváez expedition. Indeed,

Fernández de Oviedo—who met Cabeza de Vaca twice—inserted his own version in his *Historia general y natural de las Indias*. The *Joint Report* also served Cabeza de Vaca, in the form of an outline, when in 1542 in Zamora he released *La relación*. Adorno and Pautz have scrutinized and compared the two texts. They offer an insightful commentary on what might have been left out by Cabeza de Vaca from the *Joint Report* and "his uses of memory," so to speak. They also discuss Oviedo's editorial strategies; for instance, his use of the term *naufragios* to describe the Narváez expedition, "not with the literal meaning of 'shipwrecks,' but rather the figurative one of 'disasters' or 'calamities.'" Furthermore, in a study of the various renditions of the Narváez expedition, and in a chronological analysis of the versions available by Cabeza de Vaca, Adorno and Pautz refer to yet another account, described as the *Short Report*. It was drafted in 1542 by Alonso de Santa Cruz. After attempting to extrapolate the content of the *Joint Report* from various other sources, Adorno and Pautz have also tried to understand the differences between it and *La relación* authored by Cabeza de Vaca alone and published six years later. These differences include the crossing of a river, the death of shipmates, the antecedents of travelers that joined the chronicler in his journey, and so on. After the *Joint Report*, there might have been another version of the expedition, coauthored by Cabeza de Vaca and Dorantes in 1537, but if such is the case, that version too is lost. Cabeza de Vaca most likely based his own *Relación* on the *Joint Report*, but expanded and embellished it. It has also been speculated by several scholars that, since its publication coincided with Cabeza de Vaca's tenure in the Río de la Plata, the 1542 version may have been a pirated edition, unauthorized by the chronicler, although there is little evidence of this.

It is intriguing to examine the differences between the 1542 edition and the more widely recognized 1555 edition, which, as Adorno and Pautz have put it, "was part of a larger project of memorializing Cabeza de Vaca's public life of service to his king." In a "License to Print" included in the 1555 edition, which appeared during the reign of King Philip (1543–56), it is stated that *La relación* "was an effort very beneficial to the persons who were to pass through those places [Florida and the Southwest]." Since *La relación* and *Comentarios* appeared in this edition in a single volume, the scope is really that of a full-fledged memoir. At first glance this version is more elaborate, more sophisticated, with emendations, both grammatical and stylistic. His goal appears to be to entertain, but a careful analysis shows that it is less at the level of language and more in terms of content that the two versions are distinguished. Entire passages are incorporated, such as the aforementioned one about the village of blind Indians. But this version also contains errors, among them the lack of synchronicity between the chapter headings and the content that follows. This suggests that memory, at this point, played a more substantial role, since between Cabeza de Vaca's adventures in the New World and the 1555 version at least eighteen years have gone by, and means that, as he recollects, he improvises, allowing his fancy to go free. At this point, it is fair to say that the *Chronicle of the Narváez Expedition* came closer than ever before to the novelistic mode. Whereas the draft of 1542 is an attempt to show his courage and achievements to Charles V, the 1555 version seeks to present the author in a good light so as to cleanse his reputation from the charges against him after his forays in South America. Therein lies the difference: the first is a report, the second is an engaging, persuasive act of restoration.

The earliest full-text European translations of the *Chronicle of the Narváez Expedition* were made in Italian (Gian Battista Ramusio, 1556) and French (Henri Ternaux-Compans, 1837). More recently, the volume has also been rendered in German and Russian—in 1925 and 1975, respectively. Some eight complete renditions of it into English have appeared since the nineteenth century. These, obviously, are the ones that intrigue me. Among the English translations, the first one, by Thomas Buckingham Smith, appeared in Washington, D.C. in 1851, shortly after the Mexican-American War and the signing of the Treaty of Guadalupe Hidalgo, in which Mexico ceded two thirds of its territory to the United States. This was a period of enormous expansion, in which the political idea of "Manifest Destiny" justified the growth of land decades seen as undesirable only fifty years before. The publication of the account by Cabeza de Vaca allowed for a recognition—and, as such, for an epistemological appropriation—of the newly possessed geographical area. But the research done by the translator went beyond: Buckingham Smith was the first to collect biographical information about the explorer, to propose his exact landing site in Florida and to map out his trans-Texas route, to locate the Indian ranges along the northern Gulf of Mexico shore, and, finally, to identify, in preliminary format, the flora and fauna described in the volume. These endeavors are a display of the age of research into the pre-Anglo past in Florida and the Southwest in which Buckingham Smith participated, with a clear mission in mind: to show that the freshly added territories to the American chart, to be fully integrated, needed to be interpreted through the lens of English-language American historiography.

Interestingly, the next English rendition, by Fanny Ritter Bandelier, appeared shortly after the Spanish-American War, when Spain, its imperial dreams finally debunked, was forced to cede its dominion in the Caribbean Basin. This was another crucial period of Anglo-Hispanic relations, one in which, again, historians and intellectuals in the United States made sense of political gains achieved by military means through an interpretation—a debunking, really—of the Spanish colonial age. The year of publication of Bandelier's version, released in New York by the publisher A. S. Barnes, is 1904 (even though the introduction is dated March 28, 1905). This edition included a prologue by her husband, Adolph Francis Alphonse Bandelier (1840–1914), the pioneer American anthropologist of the pre-Columbian and Hispanic periods in the Americas, with important publications on the Zuñis and Pueblo Indians of the Southwest. A contemporary of Henry Lewis Morgan, he was responsible for, among other titles, *The Discovery of New Mexico by the Franciscan Monk Friar Marcos de Niza In 1539* and *Indians of the Rio Grande Valley* (coauthored with Edgar L. Hewett). As for Fanny Bandelier, she was born in Zurich in 1869 and raised there and in Lima, Peru, and, under the tutelage of her husband, became a research anthropologist and teacher who specialized in the cultural history of South America and southwestern North America. She was also the translator of Bernardino de Sahagún's *A History of Ancient Mexico*, as well as a collaborator on Charles Wilson Hackett's edition of *Historical Documents Relating to New Mexico, Nueva Vizcaya and Approaches Thereto, to 1773*.

Bandelier's rendition of *La relación* was supposedly based on the 1542 edition by Cabeza de Vaca. (Adolph Bandelier is infuriatingly unclear about this topic in his introduction, even though a close reading suggests it is indeed that version that served as the source and not its 1555 counterpart.) However, the translation does include some passages from the later edition, so much so that on numerous occasions it feels like a combination of the two. In my copy, published in New York by Allerton Book Co., Adolph traces the pattern of Cabeza de Vaca's life, minimizing his contribution and that of his companions. As "an episode," he says, it is "important, but an incident brought about by a disastrous failure." He thus stresses his anthropological interest: "A perusal of the narrative shows that the forlorn wanderers were *not*—as it has long been admitted—the 'discoverers of New Mexico.' They never saw, nor do they claim to have seen, any of the so-called 'Pueblo.' They only heard of them, in a more or less confused manner." Indeed, Adolph Bandelier time and again accuses Cabeza de Vaca of chaotic thinking. He claims that his account might prove to have ethnographic value, but that his descriptions are not to be trusted. He concludes with a word of caution about the translations of Cabeza de Vaca into English. The narrative, Bandelier claims,

> is very difficult to translate for the reason, that the criticism by Oviedo about its lack of clearness is too well founded. Many parts of chapters and also whole chapters are so confused that it is impossible to follow the original more than remotely, and paraphrasing had to be resorted to. Even then, in several instances, the meaning remains possibly somewhat obscure. It is as if the author, in consequence of long isolation and constant intercourse with people of another speech, had lost touch with his narrative tongue.

Again, Adolph Bandelier's comment ought to be seen against the larger historical background. It belongs, unquestionably, to those that feed the myth of *el español desconfiable*—"the untrustworthy Spaniard." Walt Whitman's epigraph, which opens this introduction, states the obvious in a lucidly prophetic voice: the knowledge that most Americans have of the Spanish elements of the nation's past is ridiculously—I would say shamefully—limited. This complaint, of course, is heard time and again in intellectual circles. The following quote, a confirmation of this complaint, is from *In the American Grain* (1925), by doctor and poet William Carlos Williams:

History, history! We fools, what do we know or care? History begins for us with murder and enslavement, not with discovery. No, we are not Indians but we are men of their world. The blood means nothing; the spirit, the ghost of the land moves in the blood, moves the blood. It is we who ran to the shore naked, we who cried, "Heavenly Man!" These are the inhabitants of our souls, our murdered souls that lie . . . agh. Listen! I tell you it was lucky for Spain the first ship put its men ashore where it did. If the Italian had landed in Florida, one twist of the helm north, or among the islands a hair more to the south; among the Yamasses with their sharpened bones and fishspines, or among the Caribs with their poisoned darts—it might have begun differently.

During the twentieth century, six other English translations of *Chronicle of the Narváez Expedition* were released. Those by José B. Fernández and Martín A. Favata (1993) and Frances M. López-Morillas (1993) appeared as part of the festivities of the five-hundredth controversial celebration of Columbus's arrival in the Bahamas. Their agenda, evident in the ethos that informs the translation as well as in the introductions that precede them, is to somehow set the record straight. While they present a picture of Cabeza de Vaca as a disoriented conquistador, part of a bunch that, as Fernández and Favata put it, were "neither learned scholars nor creators of beauty" but "were filled with creative power," they also insert his adventure into the larger spectrum of ethnic history within the United States. Somehow, he is presented as a forerunner of the Latino population that, in the last quarter of the twentieth century, became recognized as an increasingly essential component of the American social tapestry. The translation by Adorno and Pautz (1999) crowned this effort by showcasing scholarship as proof that north and south are intricately connected in the American continent, and that the root of their connection is the Spanish effort of exploration in the early 1530s and onward. In short, in comparison with those of Buckingham Smith and Bandelier, these more recent English renditions, especially those published in 1993, were an enticement to look at the past with "objective" eyes again, to reconsider the nation's history through a kaleidoscopic viewpoint that opens up the landscape to Whitman's sense of collective memory where the Iberian past is not a casualty but an integral component.

Each translation, hence, has promoted its own catalogue of (mis)interpretations. And so does each reader that comes to Cabeza de Vaca anew. He was, it seems to us at the dawn of this millennium, an imperfect explorer: clumsy, misinformed, dishonest even. *La relación* might be closer to fantasy than to history. But therein lies its true quality, at least in our current perspective, for is there truly a way to separate fact from fiction, especially when the author purports to present a view of himself? Invariably, memoirs and *testimonios* are subjective accounts: they falsify through enchantment and persuasion. This doesn't diminish their value in any way. The *Chronicle of the Narváez Expedition* is invaluable precisely because it is polemical. It is, has been, and is likely to remain, a point of departure whereby to rethink the Spanish quest of exploration through Florida and the Southwestern territories and the way in which readers have interpreted it to satisfy their own needs. Cabeza de Vaca engages in sexual liberty and in destruction, becomes a slave, and witnesses acts of cannibalism (though not by the natives). What he never gives up, though, is his faith in God and the sense that his acts are groundbreaking and that future generations need to find out about them. His descent to hell is our ascent to meaning. His nakedness—*su desnudez*—is an excuse for generations of readers to dress him up according to the needs of the time.

—Ilan Stavans

SUGGESTED FURTHER READING

ORIGINAL EDITIONS OF THE CHRONICLE

Cabeza de Vaca, Alvar Núñez. *Relación que dió Alvar Núñez Cabeza de Vaca de lo acaesido en las Indias en la armada donde iva por governador Pánfilo de Narvaez* . . . Zamora, Spain: Agustín de Paz y Juan Picador, 1542.

——. *La relación y comentarios del gouernador Alvar núñez cabeça de vaca de lo acaescido en las dos jornadas que hizo a las Indias.* Valladolid, Spain: 1555.

SELECTED SPANISH EDITIONS

Barrera, Trinidad, ed. *Naufragios.* Madrid: Alianza Editorial, 1985. Favata, Martin A., and José B. Fernández, ed. *La relación: o, Naufragios.* Potomac, Md.: Scripta Humanistica, 1986. Ferrando, Roberto, ed. *Naufragios y Comentarios.* Madrid: Historia 16, 1984. Maura, Juan Francisco, ed. *Naufragios.* Madrid: Cátedra, 1998. Peña, Enrique, ed. *Relación de Alvar Núñez Cabeza de Vaca.* Buenos Aires: Jacobo Pauser, 1907. Pupo-Walker, Enrique, ed. *Los naufragios.* Madrid: Editorial Castalia, 1992. Sánchez, Luis Alberto, ed. *Naufragios y Comentarios.* Mexico: Premiá Editores, 1969. Vedia, Enrique, ed. *Naufragios de Alvar Núñez Cabeza de Vaca y relación de la jornada que hizo a la Florida con el adelantado Pánfilo de Narvaez.* Madrid: Imprenta y Esterotipia de M. Rivadeneyra, 1852.

SELECTED ENGLISH TRANSLATIONS

Adorno, Rolena, and Patrick Charles Pautz, ed. *Alvar Núñez Cabeza de Vaca: His Account, His Life, and the Expedition of Pánfilo de Narváez.* 3 vols. Lincoln, Neb. University of Nebraska Press, 1999. Bandelier, Fanny, trans. *The Journey of Alvar Núñez Cabeza de Vaca, and His Companions from Florida to the Pacific, 1528–36* (includes the report of Father Marcos de Niza and a letter from the Viceroy Mendoza). New York: A. S. Barnes, 1904. ———. *The Narrative of Alvar Núñez Cabeza de Vaca.* (with Oviedo's version of the lost *Joint Report* presented to the Audiencia of Santo Domingo). Translated by Gerald Theisen. Barre, Mass.: Imprint Society, 1972. Covey, Cyclone, trans. *Cabeza de Vaca's Adventures in the Unknown Interior of America.* New York: Collier Books, 1961. ———. *Adventures in the Unknown Interior of America.* Albuquerque, N.M.: University of New Mexico Press, 1984. Favata, Martin A., and José B. Fernández, ed. *The Account: Alvar Núñez Cabeza de Vaca's Relación.* Houston: Arte Publico Press, 1993. Hakluyt Society, trans. *The Conquest of the River Plate: 1535–1555.* Vol. 2, *The Commentaries of Alvar Núñez Cabeza de Vaca.* London: Hakluyt Society, 1891. From the original Spanish edition of 1555. Hallenbeck, Cleve. *Alvar Núñez Cabeza de Vaca: The Journey and Route of the First European to Cross the Continent of North America, 1534–1536.* Glendale, Calif.: The Arthur H. Clark Company, 1940. Hodge, Frederick, with Theodore H. Lewis. *The Narrative of Alvar Núñez Cabeça de Vaca.* In *Spanish Explorers in the Southern United States, 1528–1543: The Narrative of Alvar Nuñez Cabeza de Vaca,* translated by Thomas Buckingham Smith. New York: Charles Scribner's Sons, 1907. Pupo-Walker, Enrique, ed. *Castaways.* Translated by Frances M. López-Morillas. Berkeley: University of California Press, 1993. Smith, Thomas Buckingham, trans. *The Narrative of Alvar Núñez Cabeça de Vaca.* Washington, D.C.: 1951. ———. *Relation of Alvar Núñez Cabeza de Vaca.* New York: J. Munsell, 1871.

CRITICAL STUDIES

Adorno, Rolena, "The Negotiation of Fear in Cabeza de Vaca's *Naufragios.*" *Representations* 33 (1991): 163–99. In *New World Encounters,* edited by Stephen Greenblatt, 48–84. Berkeley: University of California Press, 1993.
———. "Peaceful Conquest and Law in the *Relación* (Account) of

Alvar Núñez Cabeza de Vaca." In *Coded Encounters: Writing, Gender, and Ethnicity in Colonial Latin America*, edited by Francisco Javier Cevallos-Candau et al., 75–86. Amherst, Mass.: University of Massachusetts Press, 1994.

Ahern, Maureen. "The Cross and the Gourd: The Appropriation of Ritual Signs in the *Relación* of Alvar Núñez Cabeza de Vaca and Fray Marcos de Niza." In *Early Images of the Americas*, edited by Jerry M. Williams and Robert E. Lewis, 215–44. Tucson: University of Arizona Press, 1993.

Belloguín, Andrés García. *Vida y hazañas de Alvar Núñez Cabeza de Vaca*. Madrid: Editorial Voluntad, 1928.

Bishop, Morris. *The Odyssey of Cabeza de Vaca*. New York: The Century Co., 1933.

Carreño, Antonio. "*Naufragios* de Alvar Núñez Cabeza de Vaca: Una retórica de la crónica colonial." *Revista Iberoamericana* 53 (July–September 1987): 499–516.

Chipman, Donald E. "In Search of Cabeza de Vaca's Route across Texas: An Historical Survey." *Southwestern Historical Quarterly* 91 (1987): 127–48.

Coopwood, Bethl. "The Route of Cabeza de Vaca." *Texas State Historical Association Quarterly* 3 (1899–1900): 108–40, 177–208, 229–64; 4 (1900–01): 1–32.

González, Alejandro Acosta. "Alvar Núñez Cabeza de Vaca: Náufrago y huérfano." *Cuadernos Americanos* 9, 1 (1995): 165–99.

Hanke, Lewis. *Aristotle and the American Indians*. Bloomington, Ind., and London: Indiana University Press, 1975.

Lacalle, Carlos. *Noticia sobre Alvar Núñez Cabeza de Vaca: Hazañas americanas de un caballero andaluz*. Madrid: Instituto de Cultura Hispánica, 1961.

Lafaye, Jacques. "Los milagros de Alvar Núñez Cabeza de Vaca (1527–1536)." In *Mesías, cruzadas y utopías: El judeo-cristianismo en las sociedades hispánicas*, 65–84. Mexico: Fondo de Cultura Económica, 1984.

Lewis, Robert E. "Los Naufragios de Alvar Núñez: Historia y ficción." In *Revista Iberoamericana* 48, 120–121 (July/December 1982): 681–94.

Long, Daniel. *Interlinear to Cabeza de Vaca: His Relations from Florida to the Pacific, 1528–1536*. Santa Fe: Writers' Editions, Inc., 1939.

de Madariaga, Salvador. *The Rise of the Spanish American Empire*. New York: The Free Press, 1947.

Maura, Juan Francisco. "Veracidad en los Naufragios: la técnica narrativa de Alvar Núñez Cabeza de Vaca." *Revista Iberoamericana* 61 (1965): 187–95.

Molloy, Sylvia. "Alteridad y reconocimiento en los *Naufragios* de Alvar Núñez Cabeza de Vaca." *Nueva Revista de Filología Hispánica* 35 (1987): 425–49.

Morrison, Samuel Eliot. *The European Discovery of America*. 2 vols. New York: Oxford University Press, 1971–74.

Pastor, Beatriz. *Discursos narrtivos de la conquista: Mitificación y emergencia*. Hanover, New Hampshire: Ediciones del Norte, 1988.

Pupo-Walker, Enrique. "Pesquisas para una nueva lectura de los *Naufragios* de Alvar Núñez Cabeza de Vaca." *Revista Iberoamericana* 53 (July–September, 1987): 517–39.

———. "Sobre el legado retórico de los *Naufragios* de Alvar Núñez Cabeza de Vaca." *Revista de Estudios Hispánicos*, Puerto Rico (1992): 75–78.

Rodman, Maia. *Odyssey of Courage: The Story of Alva Núñez Cabeza de Vaca*. New York: Atheneum, 1965.

de Sopranis, Hipólito Sando. "Datos para el estudio de Alvar Núñez Cabeza de Vaca." *Revista de Indias* 27 (1947): 69–102.

Spitta, Silvia. "Chamanismo y cristianidad: Una lectura lógica intercultural de los *Naufragios* de Cabeza de Vaca." *Revista de Crítica Literaria Latinoamericana* 19, 38 (1993): 317–30.

Stavans, Ilan. *Imagining Columbus: The Literary Voyage*. New York: Palgrave, 1992, 2001.

———. *The Hispanic Condition*. New York: HarperCollins, 1996, 2001.

———. *The Oxford Book of Latin American Essays*. New York and London: Oxford University Press, 1997.

Swan, Gladys. "Do You believe in Cabeza de Vaca?" *Kenyon Review* 12 (1990): 151–59.

Wagner, Henry R. *The Spanish Southwest 1542–1794*. Albuquerque: The Quivira Society, 1937.

Weber, David J. *The Spanish Frontier in North America*. New Haven: Yale University Press, 1992.

1485–1492   Alvar Núñez Cabeza de Vaca is born in Jerez de la Frontera, Spain. This is a period of intense transformation in the nation: the Jews are expelled from the Iberian peninsula by the Catholic royalty, Isabella of Castille and Ferdinand of Aragón; Christopher Columbus sails across the Atlantic to land in the so-called New World; and Antonio de Nebrija, of Salamanca, publishes the first grammar of the Spanish language.

1503–27   Cabeza de Vaca works for four different dukes of Medina Sidonia. The scattered biographical records of this period show him as loyal and perspicacious and offer a glimpse of his voyeurism. He fights in Bologna and Ravenna in 1512, on the side of the Catholic royalty, and in support of Pope Julius II. Finally, in this period the chronicler participated in the repression of the *comunero* movement. Probably around 1520 Cabeza de Vaca marries María Marmolejo, a descendant of a *converso* family.

1527–36   The *Adelantado* Pánfilo de Narváez embarks on an expedition to Florida. Cabeza de Vaca serves as treasurer. After a power struggle, Cabeza de Vaca takes his own route. He survives shipwrecks and other natural and human disasters, and along with three other Spaniards—the Moroccan slave, Estevanico, as well as Andrés Dorantes and Alonso de Castillo Maldonado—he wanders from Florida to Texas, New Mexico, Arizona, and finally to northern Mexico. The journey places him in landscapes previously unseen by any European, and also exposes him to numerous native tribes, which he describes in his chronicle, drafted in 1542 and popularly known as *La relación*.

1537–40   Cabeza de Vaca returns to Spain. Soon after, the first version of *La relación*, printed in Zamora, circulates, generating much interest among readers and especially among explorers, he is named *Adelantado* to the River Plate, located today between Argentina and Uruguay. On November 2, 1540, he sails to South America.

1541–44   He exercises his duties as *Adelantado* in the River Plate. Eventually, though, his compatriots plot to bring him down and Cabeza de Vaca is arrested on charges of corruption and is in jail for more than a year. He is returned to the Iberian Peninsula in chains on March 7, 1545.

1545   A legal case against Cabeza de Vaca takes place. According to his secretary, Pero Hernández, Cabeza de Vaca is imprisoned and on trial by the Corte for eight years. Eventually he is released and his reputation is restored. He writes a narrative of his years as *Adelantado* in South America, known as *Comentarios*.

1555   A joint edition of *Naufragios* and *Comentarios*, with the former slightly amended, appears in Valladolid, Spain. It is believed that Cabeza de Vaca lives in Seville at the time.

1559   Probable date of Cabeza de Vaca's death. He appears to be buried in Jerez de la Frontera, in the same monastery where some of his ancestors were laid to rest. Shortly before, England and Spain become allies in the war against France.

¶La relacion que dio Aluar nu-
ñez cabeça de vaca de lo acaescido enlas Indias
enla armada donde yua por gouernador pã
philo de narbaez desde el año de veynte
y siete hasta el año d treynta y seys
que boluio a Seuilla con tres
de su compañia.:.

Title page of the first edition (Zamora, 1542)

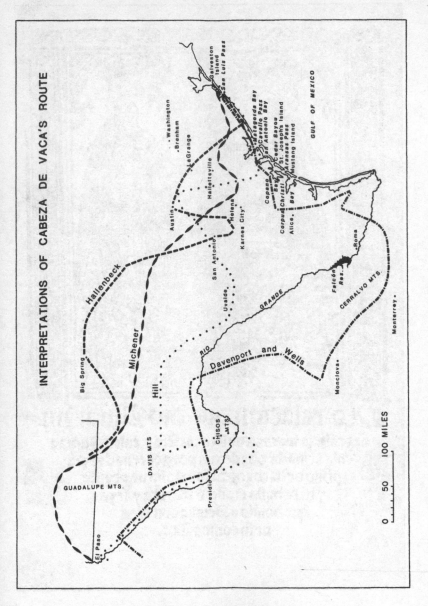

INTERPRETATIONS OF CABEZA DE VACA'S ROUTE

The Route of Cabeza de Vaca

A NOTE ON THE TEXT

The manuscripts of Cabeza de Vaca's *La relación* and *Comentarios* are located in the Archivo General de Indias and the Archivo Ducal de Medina Sidonia. This edition is based on Fanny Bandelier's English translation, which in itself is based on the 1542 edition (though with additional passages from the 1555 edition). Omitted is Adolph Bandelier's introduction and the map of North America used in it. The most complete English edition of Cabeza de Vaca's journey, in three volumes, is *Alvar Núñez Cabeza de Vaca: His Account, His Life, and the Expedition of Pánfilo de Narváez*, edited by Rolena Adorno and Patrick Charles Pautz.

This version of Bandelier's translation of *Chronicle of the Narváez Expedition* includes significant emendations. Though Alvar Núñez Cabeza de Vaca's book is an extraordinary document because of its content, its writing style poses challenges for the translator. The author frequently includes several ideas in one long "sentence," which, in itself, may be composed of a series of independent and dependent clauses that have few natural breaks, i.e., the stopping points expected by the reader when a single action or thought comes to an end. Spanish modernizations of the text have often focused on breaking these sentences down into more easily digestible thoughts. *La relación* also suffers from inconsistent spelling, rudimentary syntax, and a preponderance of the passive voice, which can give the prose a quality of tentativeness, even in descriptive passages. Some of this may have resulted from the fact that Cabeza de Vaca had few content models on which to base his writing: he was describing surroundings and experiences that had never before been set down in words, which resulted in ambiguities. On the one hand this adds to the text's literary tone. On the other, the translator is often faced with an annoying insecurity over the Spanish meaning, an uncertainty that carries over into the attempt to render it in English. Since much of Cabeza de Vaca's observations were new and there was no contemporary corroboration, it is left to the translator to uncover the historical facts underlying them.

As a specialist in the cultures and natural environment of pre-Columbian and Hispanic periods in southwestern North America and South America, Fanny Ritter Bandelier was certainly in a good position to do so. She brought to her interpretation a high degree of understanding of the cultures and physical surroundings through which Cabeza de Vaca traveled, based on her independent research. This may have helped Bandelier create a highly "readable" version. Her *Relación* does not slavishly follow Cabeza de Vaca's descriptive vocabulary, nor is she afraid to change idiomatic Spanish into idiomatic English, when doing so will make a sentence read more smoothly.

Some of her choices are puzzling, though. There were two editions of Cabeza de Vaca's chronicle during his lifetime, the first published in 1542 and the second, known as *Naufragios,* printed in 1555 in tandem with his *Comentarios.* In the introduction to his wife's translation, Adolph Bandelier claims that she followed the first edition ("This oldest print . . . has been followed exclusively in this translation."). There is ample evidence of this, including a footnote explaining a mistake in the name of one of the expedition's officers and the lack of chapter headings. However, she was also familiar with the 1555 edition, and included corrections and some of the additional passages that only appeared in the later one. Another curiosity is that even though she translated the Spanish word *tuna* correctly as "prickly pear," a word that appears thirty-five times, she chose to employ the English word only twice. In all other instances she reverted to the Spanish. Though like other modernizers she breaks Cabeza de Vaca's long sentences down into comestible parts, she also frequently follows a Spanish sentence structure, which often results in a stiff, literal translation.

In order to produce the current version, then, it was necessary to compare line-by-line the 1542 Spanish edition (resident in the collection of The New York Public Library) to Bandelier's publication. In so doing, we were able to remove the 1555 passages (we have included these elisions in the notes) as well as the Hispanic syntax and diction that sometimes affects her prose, but without changing the underlying meaning.

One emendation: in order to make the reading and textual reference easier, we have redone Bandelier's chapter divisions and headings by following the 1555 edition.

CHRONICLE OF THE NARVÁEZ EXPEDITION

The account Alvar Núñez Cabeza de Vaca gave upon re-turning to Seville[1] with three of his company of what happened between 1527 and 1536 to the fleet that went to the Indies with Pánfilo de Narváez as governor.[2]

Prologue[3]
Holy, Imperial, Catholic Majesty,

AMONG ALL THE PRINCES we have known in this world I do not believe one could be found whom men seek out with such true good will, great diligence, and desire to serve, as today we have seen them do with Your Majesty. Clearly, one is able to acknowledge here that this has not been without good cause and forethought, nor are all men so blind as to take this path blindly and without good reason. We have seen not only our own countrymen who have been obligated by faith and fealty do this, but foreigners, as well, to their own advantage. The desire and will to serve make them very much alike, except perhaps for the advantages each person will accrue.

But there is a great difference, not of their own making perhaps, but by fortune's will, or more accurately, through no one's fault, but solely through the will and judgment of God. One person ends up with greater service than he had first thought, and another finds just the opposite. The latter may be able to give no more evidence of his design than his own diligence, and even this remains at times so hidden that it remains undetected.

With regard to me and the time I spent on the mainland at Your Majesty's orders, I fully believe that my deeds and service are as plainly evident as those of my ancestors, and I have not felt the need to speak out in order to be counted among those who, with great faith and care, administer and handle the responsibilities with which Your Majesty has charged them, and honored them. But because neither my counsel nor my diligence were useful in the purpose for which we had gone in Your Majesty's service, and that, for our sins, God allowed that among all the fleets that have gone to those lands no other found itself in such danger nor came to such a miserable and disastrous end, no service is left to me but to bring an account to Your Majesty of the nine years I wandered through many very strange lands, lost and naked.[4] In this way you will know and un-

3

derstand the manner of the lands and the provinces in them, what foods and animals grow there, the customs of the many barbarous nations with which I had contact and lived, and many other details that I was able to experience and know so that in some way I will have been of service to Your Majesty. Because even though the expectations I harbored of ever leaving there were so low, the care and diligence with which I always set everything to memory was great, so that if at any time God, our Lord, wished to bring me to where I am now, I would be able to give testimony of my good will and serve Your Majesty. This account, to my mind, will be counsel of no little use to those who, in your name, may go to conquer those territories and, collectively, bring them knowledge of the true faith and true lord and service to Your Majesty. For this I have written with great surety so that even though one will read about many new things that many people will find hard to believe, they should be able to believe them without hesitation. They also should know that I have kept it brief, and I offer it to Your Majesty as it is. For this reason I ask that it be accepted in the name of service, for this is the only thing that a man who left there naked could bring back with him.

—trans. by H. A.

CHAPTER ONE

When the Fleet Left Spain and the Men Who Went with It

ON THE TWENTY-SEVENTH DAY of the month of June 1527,[5] Governor Pánfilo de Narváez departed from the port of San Lúcar de Barrameda,[6] with power and mandate from Your Majesty[7] to conquer and govern the provinces that extend from the River of the Palms[8] to the Cape of Florida,[9] which lie on the mainland. Five vessels went with him, and about six hundred men. His officers, who need to be mentioned here, were the following: Cabeza de Vaca, treasurer and chief legal officer;[10] Alonso Enriquez, comptroller; and Alonso de Solis, Your Majesty's tax agent and inspector.[11] A friar of the order of Saint Francis named Fray Juan Xuarez went as commissary,[12] along with four other monks of the order.

We arrived at the Island of Santo Domingo,[13] where we remained for nearly forty-five days, supplying ourselves with what was needed, horses in particular. Here more than 140 men of our army left us, wishing to remain as a result of the proposals and promises they had received from the people of the country.

Leaving there, we arrived at Santiago, a port on the island of Cuba[14] where, in the few days we were there, the governor resupplied himself with men, arms, and horses. A gentleman there named Vasco Porcallo,[15] a resident of Trinidad,[16] which is on the same island, offered to give the governor certain supplies he had at a distance of one hundred leagues[17] from the aforementioned harbor of Santiago.

The governor sailed in that direction with the whole fleet, but halfway there, at a port named Cape Santa Cruz,[18] he thought it best to stop and send a single ship to bring back these supplies. He ordered a certain Captain Pantoja to go with his craft and, for increased security, directed me to accompany him, while he stayed with four ships, having purchased one on the Island of Santo Domingo. When we arrived at the port of Trinidad with these two ships, Captain Pantoja went with Vasco Porcallo to the town, which is one league away, in order to take possession of the supplies. I stayed on board with the pilots, who told us that we should leave as soon as possible, since the harbor was very poor and many ships had been lost in it. Now, since what happened to us there was very remarkable, it appears to me not unsuitable for the aims and ends of my narrative to recount it here.[19]

The following morning the weather looked ominous. It began to rain, and the sea became so rough that, although I gave permission for the men to land, when they saw the weather and that the town was a league away, in order to avoid being out in the wet and cold, many came back to the ship. At the same time, a canoe came from the town bringing a letter from a person living there, begging me to come, and saying that I would be given the supplies and whatever else might be necessary.[20] I excused myself, saying that I could not leave the ships.

At noon the canoe came again with another letter, repeating the request, but with a great deal of insistence. They also brought a horse for me to ride. I gave the same reply as the first time, saying that I could not leave the ships. But the pilots and men begged me to leave in order to hasten the transfer of the supplies to the ships so that we would be able to sail soon from a place where they were very much afraid that the ships would be lost if they had to remain for much time. I decided to go, but before I went I left the pilots with instructions and orders that if the south wind should rise, which in those parts often causes ships to be lost, and they found themselves in great danger, they should beach the ships in order to save the men and horses. Then I left, wanting some of the men to accompany me. They refused, however, saying that it was too cold and rainy, and the town too far away. They promised to come, God willing, to hear mass on the following day, which was Sunday.

An hour after my departure, the sea became very rough and the north wind blew so fiercely that the small boats did not dare land, nor could the men beach the ships, since the wind was blowing from the shore. They spent that day and Sunday in great difficulty because of two contrary storms and considerable rain, until nightfall. Then the rain and storm increased in violence at the village as well as on the sea, and all the houses and the churches came crashing down. We had to lock arms and walk seven or eight men together to prevent the wind from carrying us off. It was no less dangerous under the trees than among the houses, since they were also being blown down and we were in danger of being killed underneath them. We wandered about all night in this storm and in danger, without finding anywhere we might feel safe for even half an hour.

In this plight we heard, all night long but especially after midnight, a great uproar, the sound of many voices, and a great noise of small bells, flutes, tambourines, and other instruments. Most of this noise lasted until morning, when the storm ended. Such a terrifying thing has never been experienced in these parts.[21] I took depositions about it, and sent them, certified, to Your Majesty.

On Monday morning we went down to the harbor, but did not find the ships. We saw their buoys in the water, and from this knew that the ships were lost, so we followed the shore, looking for wreckage. Not finding any, we turned into the forest. Walking through it we saw, on top of the trees a quarter of a league from the water, a small boat from one of the ships, and ten leagues further, on the coast, were two men of my crew and the tops of several crates. The men's bodies were so disfigured by having been dashed against the rocks that we could not identify them. We also found a cape and a tattered quilt, but nothing else. Sixty people and twenty horses perished on the ships. Those who went on land the day we arrived, some thirty men, were all who survived from the crews of both ships.

We remained in this state for several days, in considerable need and hardship, since the food and supplies at the village had also been destroyed, as well as some cattle. The country was pitiful to see. Trees had fallen and the woods were blighted, with neither leaves nor grass.

The situation continued until the fifth day of the month of November, when the governor arrived with his four ships. They had also weathered a great storm and had escaped by moving to a safe place in time. The people on board the ships and those he found with us were so terrified by what had happened that they were afraid to set to sea again in winter and begged the governor to remain there for the season. In view of their wishes and those of the inhabitants, he decided to winter there. He put me in charge of the ships and their crews, and I was to go with them to the port of Xagua,[22] twelve leagues away, where I remained until the twentieth day of February.

CHAPTER TWO

How the Governor Came to Xagua and Brought a Pilot with Him

AT THAT POINT the governor came with a brig he had bought at Trinidad, and with him was a pilot named Miruelo. The governor had brought the man because they said he knew the way and had been on the river of the Palms and was a very good pilot for the whole northern coast. The governor left another ship, which he had bought on the coast of Havana,[23] on which Alvaro de la Cerda remained as captain with forty men and twelve cavalry. Two days after the governor arrived he embarked again. He took along four hundred men and eighty horses, on four ships and one brigantine. The pilot we had taken with us ran the ships aground on what is known as the Canarreo shoals,[24] so that the next day we were stranded and remained stranded for fifteen days, the keels often lying on the bottom. Then a southerly storm drove so much water onto the shoals that we were able to get off, though not without considerable danger.

After leaving there, we went to Guaniguanico,[25] where another storm came up and we nearly perished. At Cape Corrientes[26] we had another, which lasted three days. Afterward we rounded the Cape of San Anton[27] and sailed against contrary winds until we were twelve leagues off Havana. On the following day, when we attempted to enter the bay, a southerly storm drove us away, so that we crossed to the coast of Florida, reaching land on Tuesday, the twelfth day of the month of April. We sailed along the coast of Florida, and on Holy Thursday, entered the mouth of a bay on that coast, at the head of which we saw several Indian lodges and dwellings.

CHAPTER THREE

How We Arrived in Florida

ON THAT DAY THE COMPTROLLER, Alonso Enriquez, left his ship and went to an island in the bay and called to the Indians, who came over and spent a good while with him. By way of trade they gave him fish and some venison. The following day, which was Good Friday, the governor left the ship with as many men as his small boats would hold. When we arrived at the Indian huts and lodges we had seen, we found them abandoned and deserted, the people having left that night in their canoes. One of the lodges was so large it could hold more than three hundred people. The others were smaller, and we found a golden rattle among the fishnets. The next day the governor raised standards in behalf of Your Majesty and took possession of the country in Your Royal name. He showed his credentials and was acknowledged as governor according to Your Majesty's commands. We likewise presented our titles to him and he complied, as was required. He then ordered the remainder of the men to disembark, along with the remaining forty-two horses, the others having perished from the great storms and the long time they had been at sea. The few that remained were so thin and weak that they would be of little use for the time being. The following day the Indians of that village arrived and, although they spoke to us, we had no interpreters and did not understand them; but they made many gestures and threats, and it seemed as if they were telling us to leave the country. With that, they left us alone, making no attempt to impede us in any way, and departed.

CHAPTER FOUR

How We Went to the Interior

AFTER ANOTHER DAY the governor resolved to go inland to explore the country and see what was there. The commissary, the inspector, and I went with him, along with forty men, among whom were six men with horses, which would be of little use. We took a northerly direction and at the hour of vespers reached a very large bay, which appeared to sweep far inland. After remaining there that night and the next day, we returned to where the ships and men were. The governor ordered the brigantine to ply the coast toward Florida in search of the port that Miruelo, the pilot, had said he knew, but he had missed it and did not know where we were or where the port was. So word was sent to the brigantine that if the port were not found, to cross over to Havana to find Alvaro de la Cerda's ship and, after taking on supplies, to come to look for us.

After the brigantine left the same men as before went inland again, with the addition of a few more. We followed the bay's shoreline and, after a march of four leagues, captured four Indians, to whom we showed corn[28] in order to find out if they knew it, for until then we had seen no trace of it. They told us that they would take us to where there was corn and they led us to their village, at the end of the bay nearby. There they showed us some that was not yet fit to be picked. We also found many cargo boxes from Castile. In each was a corpse, each corpse covered with painted deerskins. The commissary believed this to be some idolatrous practice, so he burned the crates with the corpses inside. We also found pieces of canvas and cloth, and feather headdresses that seemed to be from New Spain.[29] We also found traces of gold.

Using signs, we asked the Indians where they had obtained these things and they indicated to us that very far away there was a province called Apalache[30] in which there was a great deal of gold.

They also indicated that in that province we would find everything we held to be of value.

Once they told us about the bounty in Apalache, taking them as guides, we set out for there. After walking ten or twelve leagues, we came to another village of fifteen houses, where there was a large cultivated patch of corn almost ready for harvest, and some that was already ripe. After staying there two days, we returned to where we had left the comptroller and those from the ships and told the comptroller and the pilots what we had seen and the information the Indians had given us.

The next day, which was the first of May, the governor took aside the commissary, the comptroller, the inspector, myself, a sailor named Bartolomé Fernández, and a notary by the name of Jerónimo de Albaniz, and told us that he had in mind to move inland, while the ships should follow the coast as far as the harbor. The pilots believed and had stated that if they went in the direction of the River of Palms they would reach it soon. He asked us to give our opinions on this.

I replied that it seemed to me in no way advisable to leave the ships until they were in a safe, occupied port. I told him to consider that the pilots were at a loss, disagreeing among themselves and undecided as to what course to pursue. Moreover, the horses would not be with us in case we needed them, and, furthermore, we had no interpreter to make ourselves understood by the natives, and would not be able to converse with them. Neither did we know what to expect from the land we were entering, having no knowledge of what it was, what it might contain, and by what kind of people it was inhabited, nor in what part of it we were, and, finally, that we did not have the supplies required for penetrating into an unknown country, since of the supplies left in the ships not more than one pound of biscuit and one of bacon could be given as rations to each man for the journey. In my opinion, we should go back on ship and sail in search of a land and harbor better adapted to settlement, since the country we had seen was the poorest and most desolate ever found in those parts.

The commissary was of the opposite opinion and said that we should not go by ship, but should follow the coast in search of a harbor, since the pilots asserted that Pánuco[31] was not more than ten or fifteen leagues away and that by following the coast it was impossible to miss it, since the coast bent inland for twelve leagues. The first to arrive should wait for the others. As for going by ship, he said it would be to tempt God, after all the vicissitudes of storms, losses of men and ships, and hardships we had suffered from the time we left Castile[32] until we arrived there. His advice would be to follow the coast as far as the harbor, while the ships with the other men would follow along to the same port.

To all the others this seemed to be the best idea, except to the notary, who said that before leaving the ships they should be put into a well-known harbor, safe and in a settled country, after which we might go inland and do as we liked. But the governor clung to his own view and to the advice of the others.

Seeing his determination, I required him in Your Majesty's name not to leave the ships until they were in port and safe, and I asked the notary to testify to what I said. The governor replied that he agreed with the opinion of the other officers and of the commissary and that I had no authority to make such demands, and he asked the notary to give him a certified statement that because that country lacked the means for supporting a settlement and a harbor for the ships, he was breaking the current encampment he had established there to go in search of the port and of better land.

He then ordered the people who were to accompany him to get ready and to provide themselves with what was needed for the journey. After this he turned to me and told me in the presence of all who were there that, since I so strongly opposed the expedition into the interior and was afraid of it, I should take charge of the ships and men remaining, and in case I reached the port before him, establish a settlement there. This I declined.

After leaving there, that same day he sent me a message and begged me again to take charge of that task, saying that it seemed to him that he could trust no one else. Seeing that despite his insistence, I still declined, he asked the reasons for my refusal. I then told him that I refused to accept because I felt sure that he would never see the ships again, nor the ships him, and that seeing how utterly unprepared he was for moving inland, I preferred to share the risk with him and his people and suffer what they would have to suffer rather than take charge of the ships and thus give occasion for saying that I opposed the journey and remained with the ships out

of fear, which would place my honor in jeopardy. Under these cir-
cumstances, I would much rather risk my life than my good name.

Seeing that he was getting nowhere, he asked others to speak
with me to ask me to do it, but I gave them the same answer. Finally
he appointed as his lieutenant to remain with the ships a magistrate[33] named Caravallo.

CHAPTER FIVE

How the Governor Left the Ships

ON SATURDAY, THE FIRST OF MAY, the day on which all this had happened, the governor ordered each one of those who were to go with him to be given two pounds of ship-biscuit and one-half pound of bacon, and thus we set out upon our journey inland. We took along three hundred people. Among them were the commissary, Father Juan Xuarez, another friar named Father Juan de Palos and three priests, the officers, and forty horsemen. We marched for fifteen days, living on the supplies we had taken with us, without finding anything to eat but palmettos like those of Andalusia.[34] In all this time we did not meet a single Indian, nor did we see a house or village. At last we reached a river, which we crossed with considerable difficulty, by swimming and on rafts. Because of the swiftness of the current, it took us a day to cross. When we got to the other side, some two hundred Indians came toward us; the governor went toward them, and after he talked to them using signs, they acted in such a manner that we were obliged to attack them and seize five or six, who took us to their houses, about half a league from there, where we found a large quantity of corn ready for harvest. We gave infinite thanks to our Lord for having helped us in such great need, for, since we were new to such tribulations, we were exhausted and weak from hunger.

On the third day after we arrived, the comptroller, the inspector, the commissary, and I got together and begged the governor to send out in search of a harbor, since the Indians had told us the sea was not very far away. He forbade us to speak of it, saying it was very far indeed. Because I was the most insistent, he told me to take forty men and go on foot to find the sea and search for a port.

The next day I set out with Captain Alonso del Castillo and forty of his company. At noon we reached sandy patches that seemed to extend far inland. We walked for about one and a half leagues, with water halfway up our legs and stepping on oysters that cut our feet badly, which caused a great deal of trouble, until we reached the river we had crossed before and which emptied into the same inlet. Then, since we were poorly prepared to cross it, we returned to camp and told the governor what we had found and how, in order to explore the inlet thoroughly and find out if there was a harbor, it would be necessary to ford the river again at our first crossing point.

The next day he sent a captain named Valenzuela with sixty men on foot and six on horseback to cross the river and follow its course to the sea in search of a port. After two days he came back, reporting that he had discovered the inlet, which was a shallow bay with water to the knees, but that there was no harbor. He saw five or six canoes crossing from one side to the other, with Indians who wore feather headdresses.

After hearing this we left the next day, still searching for the province the Indians called Apalache. We took the Indians we had captured as guides, and marched until the seventeenth of June without finding an Indian who would dare to wait for us. Finally, there came to us a chief, whom an Indian carried on his shoulders. He wore a painted deerskin. Many reed-flute players preceded him and many other people followed him. He came to where the governor was and stayed an hour. Using signs, we were able to let him know that our aim was to reach Apalache, but from his gestures it seemed to us that he was an enemy of the Apalache people and that he would go and help us against them. We gave him beads and little bells and other trinkets, and he presented the governor with the hide he was wearing. Then he turned back and we followed him.

That night we reached a broad, deep river, whose current was very strong. Since we did not dare to cross it on rafts, we built a canoe and spent a whole day in getting across. If the Indians had wished to oppose us, they could easily have impeded our passage, for even with their help we had considerable trouble. One horseman, a native of Cuéllar[35] whose name was Juan Velázquez, was not willing to wait, so he rode into the stream. The strong current swept him from the horse and, when he held onto the reins, he and the animal drowned. The Indians of that chief, whose name was Dulchalchelin, found the horse and told us that we would find Velázquez further downstream, so they went after him. His death made us very sad, since until then we had not lost anybody. The horse provided supper for many that night. Having passed there, on the following day we reached the chief's village, from which he sent us corn.

That night, when the Christians went for water, an arrow was shot at one of them, but God willed that he was not hurt. The following day, we left there without any of the natives having appeared. They had all run off, but further on we saw some Indians who showed signs of hostility. Although we called to them they would neither come back or wait, but withdrew and followed behind us. The governor placed a few horsemen in ambush near the trail, who, as the Indians passed, surprised them and captured three or four, whom we kept as guides thereafter. They led us into a terrain that was difficult to cross and strange in appearance, because it had very great forests, with wondrously tall trees. So many had fallen that our path was obstructed and we had to make long detours, which caused a great deal of trouble. Many of the trees still standing were rent from top to bottom by thunderbolts, which strike very often in that country, where storms and tempests are frequent.

We traveled until the day after St. John's Day,[36] still suffering these hardships, until we came within sight of Apalache, without having been spotted by the Indians of that land. We gave many thanks to God for being so near it, since we believed what we had been told about the country and that after the long and weary march over bad trails our hardships would come to an end. We had also suffered greatly from hunger, for although we found corn occasionally, most of the time we marched seven or eight leagues without any. Besides suffering great fatigue and hunger, the backs of many among us were covered with wounds from the weight of the armor and other things they had to carry, as occasion required. But to find ourselves at last where we wished to be and where we had been assured so much food and gold would be had made us forget many of our hardships and our weariness.

CHAPTER SIX

How We Got to Apalache

ONCE IN SIGHT OF APALACHE, the governor ordered me to enter the village with nine horsemen and fifty foot soldiers, which the inspector and I undertook. Upon entering the village we found only women and children. Though the men were not there at the time, they came soon thereafter, while we were walking about, and began to fight and shoot arrows at us. They killed the inspector's horse, but in the end they left us alone and ran off.

We found plenty of ripe corn ready to be gathered and a great deal of dry corn already housed. We also found many deerskins and among them small woven blankets of poor quality, with which the women cover parts of their bodies. They had many vessels for grinding corn. The village was composed of forty small and low houses, put up in sheltered places out of fear of the great storms that continuously occur in this country. The buildings are made of straw, and are surrounded by dense timber, tall trees, and a great many ponds, in which there were so many fallen trees of such great size that they made moving about difficult and dangerous.

CHAPTER SEVEN

The Lay of the Land

THE COUNTRY BETWEEN OUR LANDING PLACE and the village and country of Apalache is mostly flat, the soil composed of sand and dirt. There are very large trees throughout and open forests containing walnut trees, laurels and other resinous types, cedar, juniper, water-oak, pines, oak, and low palmetto, like those of Castile. There are lakes everywhere, both large and small. Some are very difficult to cross, partly because they are so deep and partly because they are covered with fallen trees. They have sandy bottoms, and in the province of Apalache the lakes are much larger than those we had found previously. There are many cornfields in this province and the houses are as scattered about the country as they are in Gelves.[37] Among the animals we saw, there were three kinds of deer, rabbits and hares, bears and lions, and other wild beasts, including one that carries its young in a pouch on its belly while the young are small[38] until they are able to find their own food, and even then, when they are looking for food and people approach, the mother does not move until her little ones are in the pouch again. The country is very cold.[39] It has good pasture for cattle and there are large numbers of many kinds of birds: geese, ducks, wild ducks, muscovy ducks, ibis, small white herons (egrets), herons, and partridges. We saw many falcons, marsh hawks, sparrow hawks, pigeon hawks, and many other birds.

Two hours after we arrived at Apalache the Indians who had fled came back peaceably, begging us to give back their women and children, which we did. The governor, however, kept one of their caciques with him, which made them so angry that they attacked us the following day. They did it so swiftly and with such boldness that they were able to set fire to the lodges we occupied, but when we sallied forth they fled to the lakes nearby. Because of these and of the big fields of corn, beyond killing one Indian we could not do them any harm, except for one that we killed. The following day, Indians from a village on the other side came and attacked us in the same manner, escaping in the same way, again with the loss of a single man.

We remained at this village for twenty-five days, making three excursions during that time. We found the country very thinly inhabited and difficult to march through because of the forests, lakes, and poor trails. We asked the cacique whom we had retained and of the other Indians with us, who were their neighbors and enemies, about the land's condition and settlements, the quality of its people, about supplies, and many other things. Each answered individually, on his own, that Apalache was the largest of all the towns, that further in one encountered fewer people who were very much poorer than those here, and that the country was sparsely populated, the inhabitants greatly scattered, and that further inland one encountered big lakes, dense forests, great deserts, and wastelands.

Then we asked about the land to the south, its villages and resources. They said that in that direction, nine days' march toward the sea, was a village called Aute, where the Indians had plenty of corn, beans, and squash, and that, being so near the sea, they could get fish, and that those Indians were their friends. Seeing how poor the country was and taking into account the unfavorable reports about its population and everything else, and that the Indians continually attacked us, wounding men and horses whenever they went for water, which they could do by shooting arrows at us from the lakes where we could not reach them, and that they had killed a gentleman of Tezcuco[40] named Don Pedro, whom the commissary had taken along with him, we agreed to leave and go in search of the sea, and of the village of Aute,[41] which they had mentioned. So we left, arriving there five days later.

The first day we traveled across lakes and trails without seeing a single Indian. On the second day, however, we reached a lake that was very difficult to cross. Its water came up to our chests and had a great many fallen trees in it. When we had reached the middle, a number of Indians assailed us from behind trees that had concealed them from our sight, while others on fallen trees began to rain arrows down on us, so that many men and horses were wounded. Before we could get out of the lake, they captured our guide. After we got out, they pressed us very hard, intending to cut us off, and it was useless to turn on them for they would hide in the lake and from there wound both men and horses.

The governor ordered the horsemen to dismount and attack them on foot. The comptroller dismounted as well and our men attacked them. Again they fled to a lake and succeeded in holding the trail. Some of our men were wounded in this fight, despite their good armor. That day there were men who swore they had seen two oak trees, each as thick as a man's calf, pierced all the way through by arrows, which is not surprising if one considers the force and dexterity with which they shoot. I myself saw an arrow that had penetrated a half foot into the base of a poplar tree. All the Indians from Florida we encountered were great archers and, being very tall and naked, at a distance seem like giants. They are wonderfully built, very thin, strong, and agile. Their bows are as thick as an arm, from eleven to twelve spans long,[42] and shoot an arrow at two hundred paces with unerring aim.

From that crossing we went to another similar one, a league away, but while it was only half a league wide it was much worse. There we crossed freely and without opposition, for the Indians, having used up all their arrows at the first place, had nothing with which they would dare to attack us. The next day, while crossing at a similar place, I saw the tracks of people who had gone ahead of us, and I alerted the governor, who was in the rear, so that even if the Indians turned upon us, because we were on our guard, they would not be able to do us any harm. Once on open ground they continued to pursue us. We attacked them twice, killing two, while they wounded me and two or three other Christians, and then entered the forest again, where we could no longer harm them.

In this way we marched for eight days, without encountering any more natives, until we arrived at one league from the destination I mentioned previously. There, as we were marching along, Indians crept up unseen and fell upon our rear. A boy belonging to a nobleman named Avellaneda, who was in the rear guard, sounded the alarm. Avellaneda turned back to assist, and the Indians hit him with an arrow on the edge of the cuirass, piercing his neck almost completely through, so that he died on the spot, and we carried him to Aute. It took us nine days to get from Apalache to our stopping place. There we found that all the people had left and the lodges were burned, but there was plenty of corn, squash, and beans, all nearly ripe and ready for harvest. We rested there for two days.

After this the governor entreated me to go in search of the sea, since the Indians said it was so nearby, and we had, on this march, already suspected its proximity from a great river to which we had given the name of the Rio de la Magdalena.[43] On the following day I left in search of it, accompanied by the commissary, Captain Castillo, Andrés Dorantes, seven men on horseback, and fifty foot soldiers. We marched until sunset, reaching an inlet or arm of the sea, where we found plenty of oysters on which the men feasted, and we gave many thanks to God for bringing us there.

The next day I sent twenty men to reconnoiter the coast and explore it, who returned on the following day at nightfall, saying that these inlets and bays were very large and went so far inland that they would greatly hamper our explorations, and that the coast was still a great distance away. Hearing this and considering how ill-prepared we were for the task, I returned to the governor. We found him sick, along with many others. Indians had attacked them the previous night, putting the men in severe difficulty because of their weakened condition. The Indians had also killed one of their horses. I reported on my journey and on the poor condition of the country. We remained there that day.

CHAPTER EIGHT

How We Left Aute

ON THE FOLLOWING DAY we left Aute and marched all day to the spot I had visited on my last exploration. Our march was extremely difficult, for we had neither enough horses to carry the sick nor did we know how to relieve their suffering. They got worse every day, and to see our own deprivation caused us great pity and pain. It became obvious how few resources we had for going further and, even if we had been provided with them, we did not know where to go. Our men were mostly sick and in such bad condition that they were of little use whatsoever. I will discontinue telling this story at this point. Anyone can imagine what might be experienced in a land so foreign and evil and so utterly without resources of any kind either to stay or to leave. Nevertheless, the surest aid was God, our Lord, and we never doubted that. Then something happened that put us in a worse plight yet.[44]

Most of the horsemen began to leave in secret, hoping by this to save themselves, deserting the governor and the sick, who were helpless. Still, since among them were many men of good families and rank, they would not suffer this to happen unbeknownst to the governor and Your Majesty's officials, so that, when we reproached them, showing them at what an unseasonable time they were leaving their captain and the sick and above all abandoning Your Majesty's service, in the end they decided to stay and share everyone's fate, without abandoning one another. The governor thereupon called everyone together and asked each one individually for an opinion about this dismal country, in order to be able to get out of it and seek relief, for in that land there was none.

One third of our people were dangerously ill, getting worse by the hour, and we felt sure of meeting the same fate, which in such a country was much worse yet, since death would be our only prospect. Taking into consideration these and many other inconveniences and that we had tried many solutions, we finally resorted to a very difficult one, which was to build ships in which to leave the land. This seemed impossible to everyone, since none of us knew how to build them. We had no tools, no iron, no smithery, no oakum, no pitch, no tackling, in sum, nothing of what was indispensable. Neither was there anyone to instruct us in shipbuilding, and above all, there was nothing for those who would have to perform these tasks to eat while the work was going on. Considering all this, we agreed to mull it over. Our discussions ended for that day, and everyone went off, leaving it to God, our Lord, to put him on the right road according to his pleasure.

The next day God provided that one of the men should come and say that he would make wooden flues and deerskin bellows, and since we were in such a state that anything with the appearance of relief seemed acceptable, we told him to go to work, and agreed to make from our stirrups, spurs, crossbows, and other iron implements the nails, saws, and hatchets and other tools we so greatly needed for our purpose.

In order to get food while the proposed work was in progress we decided to make four successive raids into Aute, with all the horses and men that were fit for service, and that on every third day a horse should be killed and the meat distributed among those who worked at the boats[45] and among the sick. The raids were carried out by the men and horses that were able, and they brought in as many as four hundred fanegas[46] of corn, although not without armed opposition from the Indians. We gathered plenty of palmettos, twisting and preparing their fiber and husk and using it for the boats instead of oakum. The work on these boats was done by the only carpenter we had, and owing to great effort, progressed so rapidly that, begun on the fourth day of August, on the twentieth day of the month of September five boats of twenty-two cubits[47] were ready, caulked with palmetto oakum and tarred with pitch, which a Greek called Don Teodoro had made from some pine trees. From the husk of palmettos and the tails and manes of the horses we made ropes and tackles, from our shirts we made sails, and from the junipers that grew there we made oars, which we believed were necessary. The land into which our sins had placed us was such that only with very great difficulty could we find stones for ballast and anchors for the boats, since we had not seen a stone in the whole country. We flayed the legs of the horses and tanned the skin to make leather pouches for carrying water.

During that time some of our party went to the coves and inlets for seafood, and the Indians surprised them twice, killing ten of our men in plain view of the camp, without our being able to prevent it. We found them shot completely through by arrows, for although several wore good armor, it was not enough to protect them since, as I said before, the Indians shot their arrows with such force and precision.

According to the sworn statements of our pilots, from the bay to which we gave the name the Bay of the Cross to this place, we had traveled about 280 leagues. In this whole region we saw no mountains nor heard of any, and by the time we embarked we had lost more than forty men to sickness and hunger, besides those killed by Indians.

On the twenty-second day of the month of September we had eaten all the horses but one. We set sail in the following order. On the governor's boat there were forty-nine men, and as many in the one entrusted to the comptroller and the commissary. The third boat he placed in charge of Captain Alonso del Castillo and of Andrés Dorantes, with forty-eight men. In another he placed two captains, named Tellez and Peñalosa, with forty-seven men. The last one he gave to the inspector and me, with forty-nine men. After clothing and supplies were put on board, the sides of the boats rose a mere half a foot above the water and we were so crowded that we were unable to move. So great is the power of need that it brought us to venture out into such a troublesome sea in this manner, and without any of us having the least knowledge of the art of navigation.

CHAPTER NINE

How We Left the Bay of Horses

THE BAY FROM WHICH WE SET OUT is called the Bay of Horses. We sailed seven days among those inlets, in waist-deep water, with no sign of anything like a beach. At the end of this time we reached an island near the shore. My boat went in front, and from there we saw five Indian canoes coming toward us. When they saw us approach, the Indians abandoned their canoes and left them in our hands. The other boats continued on and they saw some lodges on the same island where we found plenty of dried mullet and their eggs, which, in our needy condition, were a very great relief. After taking them, we went further along, and two leagues beyond found a strait that we christened San Miguel, because it was that saint's day.[48] Emerging from it we reached the coast, where by means of the five canoes I had taken from the Indians we fixed the boats to some extent, making washboards and adding them to the boats to raise the sides two spans above the water.

Then we set out to sea again, plying the coast toward the River of Palms. Every day our thirst and hunger increased because our food supplies were giving out as was the water supply, since the pouches we had made from the legs of our horses soon became rotten and useless. From time to time we would enter some inlet or cove that reached very far inland, but we found them all to be shallow and dangerous. We sailed among them for thirty days, sometimes meeting Indians who were fishing and were poor and wretched people.

One night, at the end of thirty days of hugging the coast when we were in extreme need of water, we heard a canoe coming toward us. Upon seeing it we waited for it to come near, but it would not approach. Although we called out to it, it neither came forward or turned back. Because it was nighttime, we did not follow the canoe, but proceeded onward. At dawn we saw a small island where we landed to search for water, in vain since there was none. While at anchor a great storm overtook us. We remained there for six days without attempting to leave. Since it was five days since we had drunk anything our thirst was so great that we were forced to drink salt water, and several of us took such an excess of it that we suddenly lost five men.

I tell this briefly, not thinking it necessary to relate in particular all the misery and hardship we bore. If one takes into account the place we were in and the little hope of relief, one may imagine what we suffered. Seeing that our thirst was increasing and that the water was killing us, even though the storm did not abate we agreed to trust to God, our Lord, and rather risk the perils of the sea than wait there for certain death from thirst. So we went in the direction we had seen the canoe going the night we had arrived there. During that day we often found ourselves on the verge of drowning and we were so forlorn that there was no one in our company who did not expect to die at any moment.

It was our Lord's pleasure, who many a time shows his favor in the hour of greatest misfortune, that at sunset we rounded a point of land and found shelter and great improvement. Many canoes came and the Indians in them spoke to us but turned back without waiting. They were tall and well built, and carried neither bows nor arrows. We followed them to their lodges, which were nearby along the inlet, and landed there. In front of the lodges we saw many jars of water and great quantities of cooked fish. The chief of that land offered everything to the governor and led him to his home. The dwellings were made of matting and seemed to be permanent. When we entered the chief's home he gave us plenty of fish, while we gave him some of our corn, which they ate in our presence. He asked for more, so we gave more to them, and the governor presented him with some trinkets.

While we were with the cacique at his lodge, half an hour after sunset, the Indians suddenly fell upon us and upon our sick people on the beach. They also attacked the cacique's house, where the governor was, and wounded him in the face with a stone. Those accompanying him seized the cacique, but since his people were so near he escaped, leaving in our hands a robe of marten-ermine skins, which I believe are the finest in the world and give off an odor like ambergris and musk. A single one can be smelled so far off that it may seem as if there were a great many. We saw more of that kind, but none like these.

Seeing the governor hurt, those who found themselves there placed him aboard his boat and had most of the men follow him to the boats. Some fifty of us remained on land to face the Indians, who attacked three times that night so furiously that they drove us back further than a stone's throw each time.

Not one of us escaped unhurt. I was wounded in the face and if they had found a few more arrows, without a doubt they would have done us great harm. At the last onset Captains Dorantes, Peñalosa, and Tellez, with fifteen men, set up an ambush and attacked them from the rear, forcing them to flee and to leave us. The next morning I destroyed more than thirty of their canoes, which served to protect us against a northern wind then blowing, on account of which we had to stay there in the severe cold, not venturing out to sea on account of the heavy storm. After this we again embarked and sailed for three days, having taken along only a small supply of water because there were only a few containers for it, so we found ourselves in the same plight as before.

Continuing onward we entered a firth and there saw a canoe of Indians approaching. When we hailed them they came. The governor, whose boat they approached first, asked them for water. They offered to get some, provided we give them something in which to carry it, and that a Christian Greek named Doroteo Teodoro, who has already been mentioned, would go with them. The Governor and others vainly tried to dissuade him, but he insisted on going. He took along a Negro, while the Indians left two of their number as hostages. At night the Indians returned and brought back our containers, but without water or the Christians. When their people spoke to them, the ones who had remained as hostages attempted to throw themselves into the water, but our men on the boat held them back. So the other Indians left their canoe, leaving us very despondent and saddened by the loss of those two Christians.

CHAPTER TEN

On the Skirmish We Had with the Indians

IN THE MORNING many canoes of Indians arrived and demanded their two companions who had remained in the boats as hostages. The governor answered that he would surrender them provided the Indians return the two Christians. Accompanying them were five or six chiefs, who seemed to us to be of better appearance, greater authority, and superior bearing than any we had yet seen, although not as tall as those of whom we have spoken before. They wore their hair loose and very long, and were clothed in marten robes of the kind we had obtained before and which were done up in a very odd fashion because they were tied together by handsome, tawny-colored laces made of hide.

They asked us to go with them, and said that they would give us the Christians, water, and many other things. More canoes kept coming toward us, trying to block the mouth of the inlet. Because of this and because staying in this country seemed be very dangerous, we again took to sea, where we remained with them until noon. Since they would not return the Christians, we would not give up the Indians, so they began to sling stones and throw spears at us. They also threatened to shoot arrows at us, although we did not see more than three or four bows.

While we were thus engaged the wind picked up and they turned around and left us. We sailed that day until nightfall, when my boat, which was in front, came upon a promontory made by the coast. At the other end was a very large river, and at a small island on the point I anchored to wait for the other boats.

The governor did not want to land, but entered a bay close by, where there were many small islands. We got together and took fresh water from the sea there because the river emptied into it like a torrent.

For two days we had eaten corn raw, and now in order to toast it we went ashore on that island. When we did not find any firewood we agreed to go to the river, which was one league from there, behind the point. However, the current was so strong that in no way would it allow us to land. Instead, contrary to all our efforts, it carried us away from shore. The north wind that blew offshore picked up so much that it drove us back to the high sea, without our being able to do anything about it. About a half league from shore we sounded and found no bottom, even at thirty fathoms, but we could not figure out if the current was disturbing our soundings. We sailed for two more days, trying hard to reach the shore. On the third day, a little before sunrise, we saw columns of smoke rising on the coast. Working toward them, we found ourselves in three fathoms of water. It was night, however, and since we had seen so much smoke, we thought that greater danger might be lying in wait for us there, without our being aware of it nor what measures to take, so we decided to wait until morning.

By dawn the boats had been driven apart from each other. I found myself in thirty fathoms of water. Drifting along at the hour of vespers, I spied two boats. As I approached I saw that the first one was the governor's, who asked me what I thought we should do. I told him we ought to rejoin the boat ahead of us, and in no way leave her, and that the three together should continue our way wherever God might take us. He replied that that was impossible since the boat was drifting far out to sea, whereas he wanted to land, and that if I wished to follow I should set the people of my boat to their oars and to work hard at it, since only by the strength of our arms would land be reached. In this he had been advised by a captain named Pantoja, who told him that if he did not land that day he would not do so for another six, and in that time we would most likely all starve to death.

Seeing his determination, I took to my own oar and the other oarsmen in my craft did the same, and thus we rowed until nearly sunset. But because the governor had with him the healthiest and strongest men, we could in no way follow or keep up with him. Seeing this, in order to be able to follow him, I asked him to give me a rope from his boat, but he answered that it would take no small effort on their part alone to reach the shore that night. I told him that since it was barely possible for us to follow and to do what he had ordered, he should tell me what he commanded me to do. He answered that this was no time for orders; that each one should do the best he could to save himself, which is what he intended to do, and with this he went on with his craft.

Since I could not follow him, I went after the other boat, which was out at sea, waiting for me. Upon reaching it I found it to be that of Captains Peñalosa and Tellez. We traveled together for four days, our daily ration being half a handful of raw corn. At the end of these four days we were overtaken by a storm, in which the other boat was lost. God's great mercy preserved us from being drowned in that weather.

Because it was winter and the cold very great, and because we had been suffering so many days from hunger and from the injuries we had received from the waves, the next day people began to break down, so that when the sun had set all those aboard my boat had fallen in a heap and were so near dying that few remained conscious. Just five men could stay on their feet.

When night came the skipper and I were the only ones able to manage the boat. Two hours after nightfall the skipper told me to steer the craft alone, since he felt that he would die that same night. So I stood at the helm, and after midnight went to see if the skipper was dead. He said, however, that, on the contrary, he felt better and would steer till daybreak. At that point, I would have preferred to die rather than to see so many people around me in such condition. After the skipper had taken control of the boat I went to rest, very much without resting, for I thought of anything else but sleep.

Near daybreak I fancied that I could hear the sound of breakers, for since the shore was shallow, their noise was greater. Surprised about this, I called the skipper, who said he thought we were near the shore. Sounding, we found ourselves at seven fathoms, and he was of the opinion that we should keep offshore till dawn. So I took the oar and rowed along the coast, from which we were one league away, and turned the stern seaward.

Close to shore a wave took us and hurled the boat a horseshoe's throw out of the water. With the violent shock nearly all the people who lay in the boat like dead came to themselves, and, seeing we were close to land, began to crawl out on all fours. When they got out they climbed into a rocky area, where we built a fire and toasted some of our corn. We found rainwater, and with the warmth of the fire people revived and began to cheer up. The day we arrived there was the sixth of the month of November.

CHAPTER ELEVEN

What Happened to Lope de Oviedo
with Some Indians

AFTER THE MEN HAD EATEN I sent Lope de Oviedo, who was the strongest and heartiest of anyone, to go to some nearby trees and climb to the top of one to examine the surroundings and the local countryside. He did so and found we were on an island,[49] and that the ground had hollows, as if cattle had gone over it. He concluded from this that the land belonged to Christians, which he reported to us. I sent him again to look more closely to see if there were any worn trails, but not to go too far in order to avoid running into danger. He went, found a footpath, followed it for about a half league, and saw several Indian huts, which were empty because the Indians had gone out into the countryside. He took a cooking pot, a little dog, and a few mullets and turned back, but since he seemed to be delayed I sent two other Christians to look for him and find out what had happened.

They met him nearby and saw that three Indians with bows and arrows were following and calling to him, while he did the same to them, by signs. He came to where we were and the Indians remained behind, seated on the beach. Half an hour later a hundred Indian archers joined them, and our fear was so great that, whether they were tall or short, they seemed like giants to us. They stood still, close to the first ones, near where we were.

We could not defend ourselves, since only three of us could even stand up. The inspector and I stepped forward and called to them. They came, and to save ourselves we tried to calm them down as well as we could, giving them beads and bells. Each one gave me an arrow in token of friendship, and by signs they let us know that on the following morning they would come back with food, since at the moment they had none.

CHAPTER TWELVE

How the Indians Brought Us Food

THE FOLLOWING DAY, at sunrise, which was the time the Indians had told us, they came, as they had promised, and brought us plenty of fish and some roots they eat that taste like walnuts, some big, some small. Most are pulled from the water, though with a great deal of effort.

In the evening they returned with more fish and some of the same roots, and they brought their women and children to look at us. Because of the little bells and beads we had given them, they considered themselves to be very rich and thereafter visited us daily, bringing the same things as before. Since we had been provided with fish, roots, water, and the other things we had asked for, we decided to set out again and continue our voyage.

We lifted the boat out of the sand into which it had sunk, which required us to take off our clothes, and had to expend a great deal of effort to set her afloat, since our condition was such that even much lighter things would have given us trouble.

Then we set sail. Two crossbow shots from shore a wave swept over us. We all got wet, and since we were naked and the cold was very great, we dropped the oars. The next wave overturned the boat. The inspector and two others clung to her to save themselves, but the opposite happened: they ended up underneath the boat and were drowned.

Because the shore was very rough, the sea took the others and thrust them, half dead, back onto the beach on the same island, less the three that had perished under the boat. The rest of us, as naked as we had been born, had lost everything, and while it was not very valuable, to us it meant a great deal. It was November, and bitterly cold. We were in such a state that our bones could easily be counted and we looked like death itself. Of myself I can say that since the month of May I had not eaten anything but toasted corn, and even sometimes had been obliged to eat it raw. Although the horses were killed during the time the boats were built, I never could eat them and not ten times did I have fish. I say this in order to explain and so that one might have an idea of our condition. On top of all this, a north wind rose, so that we were nearer death than life. It pleased our Lord that, searching for the remnants of our former fire, we found wood with which we built big fires and then tearfully begged our Lord for mercy and the forgiveness of our sins. Everyone pitied not only himself but all the others whom we saw in the same condition.

At sunset the Indians, thinking we had not left, came to bring us food, but when they saw us in such different attire from before and of such strange appearance, they were so frightened that they turned back. I went to call them and they approached with great trepidation. Using signs, I then let them know how we had lost a boat and that three of our men had been drowned. Before them lay two of our men, dead, with the others about to end up the same way.

Upon seeing the disaster we had suffered, our misery and misfortune, the Indians sat down with us and began to weep out of compassion for our misfortune. For more than half an hour they wept so loudly and so sincerely that it could be heard far away.

In truth, to see beings so devoid of reason, uneducated, so brutish, yet so deeply moved by pity for us, increased my feelings and those of others in my company for our own misfortune. When the lament was over, I spoke to the Christians and asked them if they would like me to beg the Indians to take us to their homes. Some of the men who had been to New Spain answered that it would be unwise since, once at their homes, they might sacrifice us to their idols.

Still, seeing there was no remedy and that in any other way death was surer and nearer, I did not pay heed to what they said, but begged the Indians to take us to their dwellings. They showed great pleasure at this, telling us to wait yet a little, but that they would do what we wished. Soon thirty of them loaded themselves with firewood and went toward their lodges, which were far away, while we stayed with the others until it was almost dark. Then they took hold of us and carried us along hurriedly to where they lived.

To ward off the cold, they had provided four or five big fires on the road and at each one they warmed us, lest on the way some one of us might faint or die. As soon as they saw we had regained a little warmth and strength they would carry us to the next fire with such haste that our feet barely touched the ground.

When we got to their dwellings we saw they had built a hut for us with a great many fires in it. About an hour after our arrival they began to dance; their celebration lasted the whole night. For us, however, there was no pleasure, feast, or sleep, since we expected to be sacrificed. In the morning they again gave us fish and roots, and treated us so well that we were reassured, losing to some extent our apprehension of being sacrificed.

CHAPTER THIRTEEN

How We Learned About Other Christians

THE SAME DAY I saw on one of the Indians a trinket he had not gotten from us and, upon being asked from where they had obtained it, they answered, by signs, that other men like us, who were still in our rear, had given it to them. Hearing this, I sent two Christians with two Indians to guide them to those people, whom they met very nearby. They were looking for us as well, since the Indians had told them of our presence in the area. It was Captains Andrés Dorantes and Alonso del Castillo, with all of their crew. When they came near us they were greatly frightened by our appearance and sad that they were unable to give us anything, since they had nothing but their clothes. They stayed with us and told us how, on the fifth of that month, their boat had been stranded a league and a half from there. They had escaped without losing anything.

We agreed to repair their boat together so that those who had the strength and inclination could proceed in it while the others would remain until they were completely restored and then go as well as they could along the coast, following it till God would be pleased to get us all to a land of Christians.

So we set to work, but before the boat was afloat, Tavera, a gentleman in our company, died, and the boat proved to be unseaworthy, and soon sank. Because of our condition, which I have described, that is, most of us naked, because the weather was so unfavorable for walking and for swimming across rivers and coves, and because we had no food nor any way to carry it, we decided to submit to necessity and winter there. We also agreed that four of the most able-bodied men should go to Pánuco, which we believed to be nearby, and that, if it was God, our Lord's, will to take them there, they should give an account of our remaining on the island and of our need and distress.

One of them was a Portuguese, called Álvaro Fernández, a carpenter and sailor; the second was Méndez; the third, Figueroa, a native of Toledo;[50] the fourth, Astudilloi, from Zafra.[51] They were all good swimmers and took with them an Indian from the island of Avia.[52]

CHAPTER FOURTEEN

How Four Christians Departed

A FEW DAYS AFTER the four Christians had left, the weather became so cold and stormy that the Indians could no longer pull roots, and the canebrake in which they used to fish yielded nothing more. Since the lodges afforded so little shelter, people began to die, and five Christians quartered on the coast were driven to such extremes that they ate each other, until but one remained, who, being left alone, had no one to eat him. Their names are: Sierra, Diego Lopez, Corral, Palacios, and Gonzalo Ruiz. The Indians were so startled at this and there was such uproar among them that I truly believe if they had seen this at the beginning they would have killed them, and we all would have been in great danger. After a very short time, out of eighty men who had come there in our two parties, only fifteen remained alive.

Then the natives fell sick from a stomach ailment so that half of them died as well. They believed that we had killed them, and were, in fact, certain of it, so they agreed among themselves to kill those of us who had survived.

But when they came to execute their plan an Indian who had been keeping me told them not to believe we were the cause of these deaths, for if we had so much power we would not have allowed so many of our own people to die without our being able to cure them. He also said that there remained but very few of us, and that none of us did any harm or injury, so that the best thing was to leave us alone. It pleased our Lord they should listen to his advice and counsel and give up their idea.

We named this island the Isle of Misfortune.[53] The people we encountered there are tall and well formed; they have no other weapons than bows and arrows with which they are most dexterous. The men pierce one of their nipples from side to side, and some both of them; through this hole they thrust a reed as long as two and a half spans and as thick as two fingers; they also perforate their lower lip and insert a piece of cane in it as thin as half a finger. The women do the hard work. People stay on this island from October till the end of February, feeding on the roots I have mentioned, which they pull from under the water in November and December. They have reed-canals[54] and obtain fish only during that time; afterward they subsist on roots. At the end of February they move to other areas in search of food, because the roots begin to sprout and are not good anymore.

Of all the people in the world, they most love their children and treat them best. Should the child of one happen to die, parents and relatives bewail it, as does the whole settlement. The lament lasts a full year, day after day. Before sunrise the parents begin to weep, and then after they do so, the tribe does the same. They do it again at noon and at dusk. At the end of a year of mourning they celebrate the anniversary and wash and cleanse themselves of all their paint. They mourn all their dead in this manner, except old people, to whom they do not pay any attention, saying that these people have had their time and are no longer of any use, but only take up space and food from the children.

Their custom is to bury the dead, except those among them who are medicine men,[55] whom they burn. While the fire is burning, they all dance and have a big festival. They grind the bones to powder and, at the end of the year when they celebrate the anniversary, they scarify themselves and give the relatives the pulverized bones to drink in water.

Every man has a woman he acknowledges as his wife, but the medicine men enjoy greater privileges, since they may have two or three, and among these wives there is a great friendship and harmony. When a man takes a woman for his wife, from the day he marries her whatever he may hunt or fish, she has to take to her father's home without daring to touch it or eat it, and from the father-in-law's home they bring food to the husband. All the while neither the wife's father nor her mother enters his dwelling, nor is he allowed to go to theirs or to the homes of his brothers-in-law, and should they happened to meet they go out of each other's way a crossbow's shot or so, with bowed heads and eyes cast to the ground, because they believe it is an evil thing to look at each other or speak. The women are free to communicate with their parents-in-law or relatives and speak to them. This custom prevails from that island as far as about fifty leagues inland.

There is another custom that when a son or brother dies his household gathers no food for three months, preferring rather to starve, but the relatives and neighbors provide them with victuals. Now, since during the time we were there so many of them died, there was great starvation in most of the lodges because of their customs and ceremonials and the weather, which was so rough that those who could go out after food brought in but very little, even though they worked hard for it. Therefore the Indians who were keeping me abandoned the island and went over to the mainland in several canoes to bays where there were a great many oysters. For three months of the year they eat nothing else and drink very bad water. There is a lack of firewood but a great abundance of mosquitoes. Their lodges are made of matting and built on oyster shells, on which they sleep in hides, which they obtain only by chance.

We remained there until the end of April, when we went to the seashore, where we ate blackberries for a whole month, during which they danced and celebrated incessantly.

CHAPTER FIFTEEN

What Happened to Us on the Isle of Misfortune

ON THE ISLAND I have spoken of they wanted to make medicine men of us without any examination or asking for our diplomas, because they cure diseases by breathing on the sick, and with their breath and their hands they drive the ailment away. They summoned us to do the same in order to be at least of some use. We laughed, taking it as a joke, and said that we did not understand how to cure people.

Thereupon they withheld our food to compel us to do what they wanted. Seeing our obstinacy, an Indian told me that I did not know what I was talking about when I claimed that what he knew was useless, because stones and things growing in the field have their virtues, and he, with a heated stone, placing it on the stomach, could effect cures and take away pain, so that we, who were wiser men, surely had greater power and virtue.

At last we found ourselves in such straits that, no longer fearing any additional punishment, we had to do it. Their manner of curing people is as follows: when one is ill they call in a medicine man, and after they are well again not only do they give him all they own, but even things they strive to obtain from their relatives. All the medicine man does is to make a few cuts where the pain is located and then suck the skin around the incisions. They cauterize with fire, believing it to be very effective, which through my own experience I also found to be true. Then they breathe on the spot where the pain is and believe that by doing this the disease goes away.

The way we treated the sick was to make the sign of the cross over them while breathing on them, recite a Pater Noster and Ave Maria, and pray to God, our Lord, as well as we could to give them good health and inspire them to treat us well. Thanks to his will and the mercy he had upon us, as soon as we made the cross over them, all those for whom we prayed told the others they were cured and felt well again. They treated us well in return for having done this, and would rather be without food themselves in order to give it to us, and they gave us hides and other small things. So great was the lack of food that I often went three days without eating anything at all, which was their situation as well. It seemed to me impossible for life to go on, although I afterward suffered still greater hunger and deprivation, as I shall recount later.

The Indians who were keeping Alonso del Castillo, Andrés Dorantes, and the others who were still alive, being of another language and stock, had gone to feed on oysters at another point of the mainland, where they remained until the first of April. Then they came back to the island, which was nearly two leagues away, where the channel is broadest. The island is half a league wide and five leagues long.

All the people of this country go naked; only the women cover part of their bodies with a kind of wool that grows on trees. The girls go about in deerskins. They are very liberal toward each other with what they have. There is no ruler among them. All who are of the same descent cluster together. There are two distinct languages spoken on the island; those of one language are called Cavoques, those of the other Han. They have the custom, when they know each other and meet from time to time, to weep for half an hour before they speak. After they have wept the one who is being visited rises and gives everything he owns to the one who is visiting. The latter takes it, and in a little while goes away with it. Sometimes, after one has given and the other has gotten, they part without having uttered even a word. There are other very queer customs, but having told the principal ones and the most striking, I must now proceed to relate further what happened to us.

CHAPTER SIXTEEN

How the Christians Left the Island

AFTER DORANTES AND CASTILLO had come back to the island, they gathered together all the Christians, who were somewhat scattered. There were fourteen in all. I, as I have said, was in another place, on the mainland, where my Indians had taken me and where I suffered from such a severe illness that, although I might otherwise have entertained some hope for life, this was enough to take it away from me completely. When the Christians learned of it they gave an Indian the sable robe we had taken from the cacique, as was mentioned earlier, so that he would guide them to where I was and they could see me.

Twelve of them came, two having become so feeble that they did not dare to take them along. The names of those who came are: Alonso del Castillo, Andrés Dorantes and Diego Dorantes, Valdivieso, Estrada, Tostado, Chaves, Gutierrez, the Asturian priest,[56] Diego de Huelva, Estevanico the Negro, and Benitez. As they reached the mainland they found still another of our men named Francisco de Léon, and the thirteen went along the coast. After they had gone past us, the Indians with whom I was living told me about it, and how Hiéronimo de Alaniz and Lope de Oviedo had been left on the island.

My sickness prevented me from following or seeing them. I had to remain with the Indians from the island for more than a year. Because they made me work so much and treated me so badly I decided to escape and go to the Indians who live in the woods on the mainland, who are called the Charrucans.

I could no longer bear the life I was forced to lead. Among many other miseries, I had to pull the edible roots out of the water from among the canes where they were buried in the ground, which made my fingers so tender that the mere touch of a straw caused them to bleed. The reeds would cut me all over, because many of them were broken. I had to walk through them with the clothing I had on, which I have already recounted. This is why I made an effort to join the other Indians. Among them I improved my lot a bit by becoming a trader, doing the best I could at it, and they gave me food and treated me well.

They asked me to go from place to place to get what they needed, since owing to constant warfare there is little travel or barter in the land. Trading my wares, I went inland as far as I wished and along the coast as much as forty or fifty leagues. My stock consisted mainly of pieces of seashells and cockles, and shells with which they cut a beanlike fruit, which they use for healing and in their dances and feasts. To them, after shell beads and other objects, it holds the most value. I carried these things inland, and in exchange brought back hides and red ocher with which they rub and dye their faces and hair; flint for arrow points; glue and hard canes with which to make them; and tassels made of the hair of deer, which they dye red. This trade suited me because it gave me the freedom to go wherever I pleased. I was not bound to do anything and was no longer a slave. Wherever I went they treated me well and fed me, for the sake of my merchandise.

My principal object in doing it, however, was to find out in what manner I could proceed on my way. I became well known among them and they rejoiced greatly when they saw me since I brought them what they needed. Because of my reputation, those who did not know me desired to meet me and would make every effort to do so.

It would take me a long time to recount my sufferings while trading in this way. Danger, hunger, storms, and frost often overtook me when I was alone and in open fields, from which, through the mercy of God, our Lord, I escaped. For this reason I did not go out to trade in winter, since it was the time when the Indians themselves remain in their huts and dwellings and are unable to go out or assist each other. I spent nearly six years in this country, alone with them and as naked as they were.

The reason for my staying so long was that I wished to take with me a Christian named Lope de Oviedo, who lingered on the island. One of our other companions, Alaniz, who had remained with him after Alonso del Castillo and Andrés Dorantes and all the others had gone, soon died, and in order to get Oviedo out of there, I went over to the island every year, entreating him to leave with me and go in search of Christians as well as we could. But year after year he put it off to the following year. In the end I got him to come, took him away, and carried him across the inlets and the four rivers on the coast, since he could not swim. From there we proceeded along with several Indians to an inlet one league wide and very deep throughout, which seemed to us, from what we saw, to be the one called the Bay of the Holy Ghost.

On the opposite shore we saw Indians who had come to meet those in our company. They informed us that further on there were three men like ourselves and told us their names. Upon being asked about the rest of the party, they answered that they had all died of the cold and hunger and that the Indians beyond had killed Diego Dorantes, Valdivieso, and Diego de Huelva simply as a pastime, just because they had gone from one house to another. And their neighbors, where Captain Dorantes was now living, had, because of some dream dreamt by these Indians, killed Esquivel and Méndez, as well.

We asked them about those who were still alive. They said they were in very sorry condition, since the boys and other Indians, idlers and roughs, kicked them, slapped their faces, and beat them with sticks. Such was the life they had to lead.

We inquired about the country further on and the sustenance that might be found in it. They said it was very thinly settled, with nothing to eat. People there died of the cold, since they had neither hides nor anything else to protect them. They also told us that, if we wished to meet the three Christians about two days' journey away, the Indians would come to feed on walnuts at a place about a league from there on the shore of that river. And to show us that what they said of the ill-treatment of our people was true, the Indians kicked and beat my companion. Nor did they exempt me from my share of this treatment. They threw mud at us and put arrows to our chests every day, saying they would kill us in the same way as our other companions. Fearing this, Lope de Oviedo, my companion, said he preferred to go back with some women of the Indians in whose company we had forded the cove and who had remained behind. I insisted he not go and did all I could to convince him to remain, but in vain. He went back and I remained alone among these Indians, who are named Quevenes, whereas those with whom he went away were called Deaguanes.

CHAPTER SEVENTEEN

How the Indians Arrived with Andrés Dorantes
and Castillo and Estevanico

TWO DAYS after Lope de Oviedo had gone, the Indians who had Alonso del Castillo and Andrés Dorantes came to the very spot we had been told of to eat the walnuts upon which they subsist for two months a year, without eating anything else, grinding certain small grains with them. Even this they do not always have, since one year there may be some and the next year not. The nuts are the size of the ones from Galicia. There are many of these trees and they are very big.

An Indian told me that the Christians had come and that if I wished to see them I should run away to hide on the edge of a grove to which he pointed, since he and some of his relatives were to visit these Indians and would take me along to the Christians. I trusted them because they spoke a different language from that of my Indians and was determined to do it, so the next day they took me along. When I neared the site at which they had their lodges, Andrés Dorantes came out to see who it was, because the Indians had also told him that a Christian was coming. When he saw me he was very frightened, since for many days they thought I was dead, because the Indians had told them so. We gave many thanks to God for being together again and that day was one of the happiest we enjoyed in all our days. On the way to where Castillo was they asked me where I was going. I told them my purpose was to go to a country of Christians and that I was following that direction and trail. Andrés Dorantes said that for many days he had been urging Castillo and Estevanico to go further on, but they did not risk it because they were unable to swim and afraid of the rivers and inlets that one had cross so often in that country.

Still, as it pleased God, our Lord, to spare me after all my sufferings and sickness and finally let me rejoin them, they at last decided to escape because I would take them safely across the rivers and bays we might encounter. They advised me to in no way give the Indians any idea or let them know about the plan or they would immediately kill me. To avoid this it was necessary to remain with them for another six months, after which they would move to another area in order to eat prickly pears. These are a good-tasting, red-and-black fruit the size of eggs. For three months they eat nothing else, subsisting on them exclusively.

At the time they pick this fruit, other Indians from further on come to them to barter and exchange bows, and when they headed back we thought of joining them and escaping in this way. With this in mind, I remained, and they gave me as a slave to an Indian with whom Dorantes was living.[57] They are called Marianes, and Castillo was with others, called Yguaces, who were their neighbors.

While I was there with them, they told me that after leaving the Isle of Misfortune, on the coast they met the boat in which the comptroller and the monks were adrift, and that crossing four rivers, all of which were very large and swift, the boats in which they were traveling were swept out to the sea, where four of them drowned. Thus they went ahead until they had crossed the inlet, which they did by dint of great effort. Fifteen leagues from there they met another of our parties, and when they reached there, two of their companions had already died in sixty leagues of travel. The survivors were also very near death. On the whole trip they ate nothing but crawfish and meadow grass.

At the last cove, they said, they saw Indians eating blackberries, who, upon espying the Christians, went away to another promontory. While seeking a way to cross the cove an Indian and a Christian came toward them, and they recognized Figueroa, one of the four we had sent ahead from the Isle of Misfortune. He told them how he and his companions had come there, where two of them and one Indian had died from the cold and hunger because when they had arrived, and during their whole stay, the weather was the worst weather ever known. He also said the Indians took him and Méndez.

While he was with them Méndez ran away, going in the direction of Pánuco as best he might, but the Indians pursued and killed him. Also while he was with them they told him that there was a Christian with the Marianes[58] who had come over from the other side and had met him with those called Quevenes; and that this Christian was Hernando de Esquivel, from Badajoz, a compatriot of the commissary. From Esquivel he learned how the governor, the comptroller, and the others had ended up.

The comptroller, with the friars, had become stranded with their boat among the rivers, and, while they were proceeding along the coast, the boat of the governor and his men landed as well. The governor then went with his boat as far as the big cove, whence he returned and took his men across to the other side, then came back for the comptroller, the monks, and the rest. He told him as well that after disembarking, the governor revoked the powers he had given to the comptroller as his lieutenant, giving the office to a captain who was with him called Pantoja.

The governor did not land that night, but remained on his boat with a pilot and a page, who was sick. They had neither water nor anything to eat aboard, and at midnight such a violent northerner set in that, since they had only a stone for an anchor, the boat was carried out to sea, without anybody noticing it. They were never heard from again. The people who had remained on land proceeded along the coast, and, being much impeded by water, put great effort into building rafts, on which they crossed to the other side.

Going on, they reached a point of timber on the beach, where they found Indians, who, upon seeing them approach, placed their lodges on canoes and crossed over to the other side of the coast. The Christians, in view of the season and weather, since it was the month of November, remained in this timber, because they found water and firewood, crawfish, and other seafood, but they began to die from the cold and hunger.

Moreover, Pantoja, who remained as lieutenant, treated them badly. Because of this Sotomayor, brother of Vasco Porcallo, the one from the island of Cuba who had come in the fleet as camp master, unable to stand it any longer, quarreled with Pantoja, hit him, and he died. In this way they perished one after the other. The survivors sliced the dead for meat. The last one to die was Sotomayor and Esquivel cut him up and fed on his body until the first of March, when an Indian, one of those who had taken flight previously, came to see if they were dead and took Esquivel along with him.

Once in the hands of this Indian, Figueroa spoke to Esquivel, learned from him what we have been told here, and entreated him to go with him toward Pánuco. But Esquivel refused, saying he had heard from the monks that Pánuco was in their rear, and so he remained, while Figueroa went back to the coast where he had been before.

CHAPTER EIGHTEEN

Esquivel's Account, Related by Figueroa

FIGEROA GAVE THIS ACCOUNT by following Esquivel's narrative, and thus, from one to the other, it came down to me. Through it the fate of the whole fleet will be learned and known, and what happened to everyone in particular. He said furthermore that if the Christians would travel about in that vicinity for some time they might possibly meet Esquivel, because Figueroa knew that he had run away the Indian with whom he was living and had gone to others called Marianes, who were their neighbors. And, as I have just said, he and the Asturian wished to go to other Indians further on, but when those with whom they were living found this out they beat them severely, took away the Asturian's clothes, and stabbed him in the arm with an arrow.

At last the Christians escaped by running off and remaining with the other Indians, whose slaves they agreed to become. But, although they served them, they were so badly treated that no slaves, nor men in any condition of life, have ever been so abused. Not content with cuffing and beating them and pulling out their beards for mere pastime, they also killed three out of the six, Diego Dorantes, Valdivieso, and Diego de Huelva, merely because they went from one lodge to another. The three remaining ones expected to meet the same fate in the end.

To escape from that life Andrés Dorantes fled to the Marianes, who were the ones with whom Esquivel had been living. They told him how Esquivel had stayed with them and how he ran away because a woman dreamed he would kill her son, and the Indians pursued and killed him. They also showed Andrés Dorantes his sword, his rosary, his prayer book, and other things of his. It is a custom of theirs to kill even their own children because of dreams, and they leave newborn girls to be eaten by dogs. The reason they do it, they say, is that everyone in the country is their enemy, with whom they are constantly at war, and if they marry their daughters, their enemies may multiply so much that they will be able to overcome them and reduce them to slavery. Hence they prefer to kill the girls rather than see them give birth to children who will become their foes.

We asked them why they did not wed the girls themselves. They replied it was bad to marry their own kin, and much better to do away with their daughters than to leave them to relatives or to enemies. They share this custom with their neighbors, the Yguaces. No other tribe of that country has it. When they wish to get married they buy their wives from their enemies. The price paid for a woman is a bow, the best to be had, with two arrows, and if he has no bow an Indian gives a net as wide and long as a fathom.

Dorantes remained only a few days with those Indians and then escaped. Castillo and Estevanico went inland to the Yguaces. All of those people are good archers and well built, although not as tall as those we had left behind us, and they pierce their nipple and lip. Their principal foods are two or three kinds of roots, for which they hunt all over the land and which are very unhealthy and bloating. It takes two days to roast them, many are very bitter, and even beyond that harvesting them is difficult. But their hunger is so great that these roots so indispensable to them that they will walk two and three leagues just to gather them. Now and then they kill deer and at times catch fish, but this is rare. Their hunger is so great that they eat spiders and ant eggs, worms, lizards and salamanders and serpents, and vipers whose bite is fatal. They eat earth and wood, and anything they can get, including deer dung and other things I do not wish to mention. I truly believe from what I saw that if there were any stones in the country they would eat them as well. They keep the bones of the fish, snakes, and other animals they have eaten to pulverize them and eat the powder.

The men do not carry burdens or loads, which is done by women and old men, whom they value the least. They are not as fond of their children as the ones I spoke about before. Some of them are given to unnatural vices. The women have to work very hard in many different ways, for out of twenty-four hours of day and night they get only six hours' rest. They spend most of the night tending the ovens to dry the roots they eat and at daybreak they begin to dig and carry firewood and water to their houses and attend to other necessary matters.

Most of these Indians are great thieves, for, although they are very liberal toward each other, as soon as one turns his head his own son or father grabs what he can. They are great liars and drunkards, and drink to become intoxicated. They are so accustomed to running that, without resting or getting tired, they run from morning till night in pursuit of a deer. They kill a great many because they follow it until the game is worn out and sometimes catch it alive. Their huts are of made of matting placed over four arches.[59] They carry them on their back and move every two or three days in search of food; they plant nothing of any use.

They are a very merry people, and even when famished do not refrain from dancing and celebrating their feasts and ceremonies. Their best times are when prickly pears ripen because then they have plenty to eat and spend their time dancing and eating day and night. As long as the prickly pears last they squeeze them and open them and set them to dry. When they are dry, like figs, they are put in baskets and kept to be eaten when they travel. They grind and pulverize the peelings.

While we were with them we often went three or four days without food. Then, in order to cheer us up, they would tell us not to despair, since we would soon have prickly pears and eat a great deal and drink their juice and get great bellies and be merry and contented and without hunger. But from the day they told us this to the season of prickly pears five or six months were still to come and we had to wait that long.

When the time came and we went to eat prickly pears, there were a great number of three kinds of mosquitoes, which persecuted us during most of the summer, all of them very bad and troublesome. In order to protect ourselves we built big fires of damp and rotten wood all around our camp, which gave off no flame but a lot of smoke. This caused further trouble, for the whole night we did nothing but cry from the smoke in our eyes, and the heat from the fires was so insufferable that we would go to the shore for rest. Sometimes, when we were able to sleep, the Indians would beat us to remind us to go and tend the fires.

Those from further inland have another remedy, just as bad or even worse, which is to go around with a firebrand, setting fire to the plains and timber in order to drive off the mosquitoes, and to get lizards and similar things, which they eat, to come out of the ground. They kill deer in this manner, encircling them with fire. They do it to deprive the animals of pasture, as well, compelling them to go for food where the Indians want them to be. They never build their dwellings except where there are wood and water, and they sometimes load themselves with what they need and go in quest of deer, which are found mostly where there is neither water nor wood.

On the very day they arrive they kill deer and whatever else can be had and use all the water and wood to cook their food and build fires to combat the mosquitoes. They wait another day to get something to take along on the road, and when they leave they are so badly bitten by mosquitoes that it seems as if they had the disease of Saint Lazarus.[60] In this manner they satisfy their hunger twice or three times a year and at great sacrifice, as I have mentioned. Having been with them I can say that no toil or suffering in this world approaches it.

All over this country there are a great many deer, fowl, and other animals, which I have already recounted. Here they also encounter cows, which I have seen three times and whose meat I have eaten. They appear to me of the size of those in Spain. Their horns are small, like those of the Moorish cattle; their hair is very long. Some are brownish and others black, and to my taste they have better and more meat than those from here. From the smaller ones, the Indians make blankets to cover themselves and from the larger they make shoes and shields. These cows come from the north, across the country further on, to the coast of Florida, and are found all over the land for over four hundred leagues. All along this road, through the valleys along which they come, the people who inhabit the area come down to live off them, and a great quantity of hides can be found throughout the land.[61]

CHAPTER NINETEEN

How the Indians Separated Us

WHEN I HAD BEEN with the Christians for six months, waiting to execute our plans, the Indians went for prickly pears, at a distance of thirty leagues from there, and when we were about to run away, the Indians began fighting among themselves over a woman, cuffing and striking and hurting each other, so that each one took his lodge and went his own way in a great rage. So we Christians had to part, and there was no way we could get together again until the following year. During that time I fared very badly, as much from lack of food as from the abuse the Indians gave me. I was treated so badly that I had to flee from my masters three times, and they all went in pursuit, ready to kill me. But God, our Lord, in his infinite goodness, protected me and saved my life.

When the prickly pear time arrived we met each other again at the same spot. We had already agreed to escape and appointed a day for it, when on that very day the Indians separated us, sending each one to a different place, and I told my companions that I would wait for them at the prickly pears until full moon. It was the first of September and the first day of the new moon, and I told them that if at the set time they did not appear I would go on alone without them. We parted, each one going off with his Indians.

I remained with mine until the thirteenth of the moon, determined to escape to other Indians as soon as the moon was full, and on that day Andrés Dorantes and Estevanico arrived. They said they had left Castillo with other people nearby called Anagados and told me how they had suffered many hardships and been lost. On the following day our Indians moved toward where Castillo was. They were going to join those who were holding him and make friends with them, since until then they had been at war. In this way we got Castillo as well.

During the entire time we ate prickly pears we were thirsty. To allay our thirst we drank the fruit's juice, first pouring it into a pit, which we dug in the soil, and when that was full drinking to satisfaction. The Indians do it in that way, because they lack drinking glasses. The juice is sweet and has the color of must. There are many kinds of prickly pears, some very good ones, although to me they all tasted alike. Hunger never left me time to select or even stop to think about which ones were better. Most of the people drink rainwater that collects here and there, for, even though there are rivers, they never have a fixed dwelling place and have no knowledge of springs or established water holes.

All over the land there are vast and handsome pastures, with good grass for cattle, and it strikes me that the soil would be very fertile were the country inhabited and improved by reasoning people. We saw no mountains the entire time we were in this country. These Indians told us that further on there were others called Camones, who live nearer the coast, and that it was they who had killed everyone who had come in Peñalosa and Tellez's boat. They had been so emaciated and feeble that when they were being killed they offered no resistance, so the Indians finished them off. They showed us some of their clothes and weapons and said the boat was still beached there. This is the fifth of the missing boats. That of the governor we have already said had been swept out to sea. That of the comptroller and the monks was seen stranded on the beach and Esquivel told us of their end. Of the two in which Castillo, Dorantes, and I had been, I have recounted how they sank close to the Isle of Misfortune.

CHAPTER TWENTY

How We Fled

TWO DAYS AFTER WE MOVED we commended ourselves to God, our Lord, and fled, hoping that, although it was late in the season and the fruit of the prickly pears was giving out, by remaining in the field we might still get over a good portion of the land. As we proceeded that day, in great fear lest the Indians follow us, we spied smoke, and, going toward it, reached a place after sundown, where we found an Indian who, when he saw us coming, did not want to come toward us and ran away. We sent the Negro after him, and since the Indian saw him approaching alone he waited. The Negro told him that we were going in search of the people who had made the smoke. He answered that their dwellings were nearby and that he would guide us, and we followed. He hurried ahead to let them know of our coming. At sunset we came in sight of the lodges, and two crossbow shots before reaching them we met four Indians waiting for us, who received us well. We told them in the language of the Marianes that we had come to see them. They appeared to be pleased with our company and took us to their homes. They lodged Dorantes and the Negro at the house of a medicine man, and me and Castillo at that of some other people. These Indians speak another language and are called Avavares. They were the ones who used to bring bows to our Indians and barter with them, and, although they are of another nation and language, they understood the language of those with whom we had been and had arrived there on that very day with their lodges. They soon offered us many prickly pears, because they had heard of us and of how we cured people and of the marvels our Lord worked through us. And surely, even if there had been no other tokens, it was wonderful how he prepared the way for us through a barely inhabited country, causing us to meet people where for a long time there had been none, saving us from so many dangers, not permitting us to be killed, maintaining us through starvation and misfortune, and moving the hearts of the people to treat us well, as we shall relate further on.

CHAPTER TWENTY-ONE

How We Cured Several Sick People

ON THE NIGHT WE ARRIVED THERE, some Indians came to Castillo complaining that their heads ached and begging him for relief. At the very moment he had made the sign of the cross over them and commended them to God, the Indians said that all the pain was gone. They went back to their homes and brought us a number of prickly pears and a piece of venison, which we did not recognize. As the news spread that same night there came many other sick people for him to cure, and each brought a piece of venison, and there were so many that we did not know where to store the meat. We thanked God for his mercy and kindness, which increased daily, and after they were all well they began to dance and celebrate and feast until sunrise of the following day.

They celebrated our coming for three days, at the end of which we asked them about the land further on, the people we might meet there, and the food we might find. They replied that there were plenty of prickly pears all through that country, but that the season was over and nobody was there because they had all gone home after gathering prickly pears and that the country was very cold and had very few hides in it. Hearing this, and since winter and its cold weather were setting in, we decided to spend it with those Indians. Five days after our arrival they left to get more prickly pears where there were people of other nations and languages. We traveled for five days, during which we suffered greatly from hunger since on the way there were neither prickly pears nor any kind of fruit, until we came to a river, where we pitched our lodges.

As soon as we were settled we went out to hunt for the fruit of a certain type of tree, which is like spring bitter vetch. Since throughout that land there are no paths, I took too much time hunting for them and the people went back without me. That night, as I started to rejoin them, I went astray and got lost. It pleased God to let me find a burning tree, by the fire of which I spent that very cold night, and in the morning I loaded myself with wood, taking two burning sticks, and continued my journey. Thus I went on for five days, always with my firebrands and load of wood, so that in case the fire went out where there was no timber, since in many parts there is none, I would always have the means to make other torches and not be without firewood. It was my only protection against the cold, for I was as naked as the day I was born. For the night I used the following artifice.

I went to the brush in the timber near the rivers and stopped in it every evening before sunset. Then I scratched a hole in the ground and threw a great deal of firewood from the numerous trees in it. I also picked up fallen dry wood and built four fires crosswise around the hole, being very careful to stir them from time to time. I made bundles from the long grass that grows there, with which I covered myself in the hole and so was protected from the night cold. One night fire fell on the straw covering me, and while I was asleep in the hole, it began to burn so rapidly that, although I hurried out as quickly as possible, I still have marks on my hair from this dangerous accident. During all that time I did not eat a mouthful, nor could I find anything to eat, and my feet, because they were bare, bled a great deal. God had mercy upon me, that in all this time there was no norther or I could not have survived.

At the end of five days I reached the bank of a river and met my Indians. They, as well as the Christians, had given me up for dead, thinking that perhaps some snake had bitten me. They all were greatly pleased to see me, the Christians especially, and told me that thus far they had wandered about famished and therefore had not hunted for me, and that night they gave me some of their prickly pears. On the next day we left and went where we found a great number of that fruit with which everyone satisfied their hunger, and we gave many thanks to our Lord, whose help to us never failed.

CHAPTER TWENTY-TWO

How the Following Day They Brought Other Sick People

EARLY THE NEXT DAY many Indians came and brought five people who were paralyzed and very ill and who had come for Castillo to cure them. Each patient offered him his bow and arrows, which Castillo accepted, and by sunset he had made the sign of the cross over each of the sick people, commending them to God, our Lord. We all prayed to him as well as we could to restore them to health and he, seeing there was no other way of getting those people to help us so that we might be saved from our miserable existence, had mercy on us. In the morning they all woke up well and hearty and went away in such good health that it was as if they never had had any ailment at all. This created great admiration among them and moved us to thank our Lord and to greater faith in his goodness and the hope that he would save us, guiding us to where we could serve him. For myself I may say that I always had full faith in his mercy and that he would liberate me from captivity, and I always told my companions so.

When the Indians had gone with their now healthy Indians, we moved on to others called Cultalchulches and Maliacones, who speak a different language and who were eating prickly pears as well. With them were still others, called Coayos and Susolas, and in another area were the Atayos, who were at war with the Susolas and exchanged arrow shots with them every day.

In this whole country, nothing was spoken of but the wonderful mysteries that God, our Lord, performed through us. They came from far and wide to be cured, and after having been with us two days, some of the Susolas begged Castillo to go and attend to a man who had been wounded, as well as to others that were sick and among whom, they said, was one who was on the verge of death. Castillo was very fearful, especially in frightening and dangerous cases, always afraid that his sins might interfere and prevent the cures from being effective. Therefore the Indians told me to go and perform the cure. They liked me. They remembered that I had cured them while they were out gathering walnuts, for which they had given us walnuts and hides, which had taken place at the time I was on my way to join the Christians. So I had to go, and Dorantes and Estevanico went with me.

When I got close to their huts I saw that the sick man we had been called to cure was dead, for there were many people around him weeping and his lodge was torn down, which is a sign that the owner has died. I found the Indian with his eyes rolled back, without pulse and with all the marks of death, at least it seemed so to me, and Dorantes said the same thing. I removed the mat with which he was covered, and as best I could I prayed to our Lord to restore him to health as well as any others in need. After I had made the sign of the cross and breathed on him many times, they brought his bow and presented it to me, as well as a basket of ground prickly pears, and then they took me to many others who were suffering from sleeping sickness. They gave me two more baskets of prickly pears, which I left for the Indians that had come with us. Then we returned to our living quarters.

Our Indians, to whom I had given the prickly pears, remained. At night they returned, saying that the dead man whom I attended to in their presence had resuscitated, risen from his bed, walked about, eaten, and talked to them, and that everyone I had treated was well and in very good spirits. This caused great surprise and awe, and all over the land nothing else was spoken of. Everyone who heard about it came to us so that we might cure them and bless their children. When the Cultalchulches, who were in the company of our Indians, had to return to their country, before parting they offered us all the prickly pears they had for their journey, not keeping a single one. They gave us flint stones as long as one and a half palms, which are greatly prized among them and with which they cut. They begged us to remember them and pray to God to keep them healthy always, which we promised to do. Then they left, the happiest people on earth, having given us the very best of what they owned.

We remained with the Avavares for eight months, according to our reckoning of the moons. During that time people came to us from far and wide and said that we were truly the children of the sun. Until then Dorantes and the Negro had not cured anyone, but we found ourselves so pressed by the Indians coming from all sides that all of us had to become medicine men. I was the most daring and reckless of all in undertaking cures. We never treated anyone that did not afterward say he was well, and they had such confidence in our skill that they believed that none of them would die as long as we were among them.

These Indians and the ones we left behind told us a very strange tale. From their account it may have occurred fifteen or sixteen years ago. They said that at that time there wandered about the country a man whom they called "Bad Thing," who was short and bearded. Although they could never see his features clearly, whenever he would approach their dwellings their hair would stand on end and they would begin to tremble. In the doorway of the lodge a firebrand would then appear. The man would come in and take hold of anyone he chose. With a sharp knife made of flint, as broad as a hand and two palms in length, he would then make a cut in that person's flank, thrust his hand through the gash, and take out the person's entrails. Then he would cut off a piece one palm long, which he would throw into the fire. Afterward he would make three cuts in one of the person's arms, the second one at a place where people are usually bled, and twist the arm, but would reset it soon afterward. Then he would place his hands on the wounds, which, they told us, would close up at once. Many times he appeared among them while they were dancing, sometimes in the dress of a woman and other times as a man, and whenever he took a notion to do it he would seize a hut or lodge, take it up into the air, and come down with it again with a great crash. They also told us how, many a time, they set food before him, but he would never partake of it. When they asked him where he came from and where he had his home, he pointed to a rent in the earth and said his house was down below.

We laughed a great deal at those stories and made fun of them. Seeing our disbelief they brought us many of those he had taken, they said, and we saw the scars from his slashes in the places they had said. We told them he was a demon and explained as best we could that if they would believe in God, our Lord, and be Christians like ourselves, they would not have to fear that man, nor would he come and do these things to them, and they might be sure that as long as we were in this country he would not dare to appear again. This pleased them greatly and they lost much of their apprehension.

The same Indians told us they had seen the Asturian and Figueroa with other Indians from further along the coast whom we had named the People of the Figs. None of them know how to reckon the seasons by either sun or moon, nor do they count by months and years; they judge the seasons by the ripening of fruit, by the time that fish die, and by the appearance of the stars, and in all of this they are very clever and expert. While with them we were always well treated, although our food was never too plentiful, and we had to carry our own water and wood. Their dwellings and their food are like those of the others we had known, but they are much more prone to hunger, having neither corn nor acorns or walnuts. We always went naked like them and at night covered ourselves with deerskins.

During six of the eight months we were with them we suffered greatly from hunger, because they do not have fish either. At the end of that time the prickly pears began to ripen. Without their noticing it the Negro and I left and went to other Indians further ahead, called Maliacones, at a distance of one day's travel. Three days after we arrived I sent him back to get Castillo and Dorantes, and after they rejoined me we all departed in company of the Indians, who went to eat a small fruit of a certain type of tree, on which they subsist for ten or twelve days, until the prickly pears are fully ripe. There they joined other Indians called Arbadaos, whom we found to be so sick, emaciated, and bloated that we were greatly astonished. The Indians with whom we had come went back on the same trail, and we told them that we wished to remain with the others, which made them sad. So we remained with the others in a field near their dwellings.

When the Indians saw us, they gathered together and, after having talked among themselves, each one took the one of us he had claimed by the hand and led us to their homes. While we were with them we suffered more from hunger than we had with any of the others. In the course of a whole day we did not eat more than two handfuls of the fruit, which was green and contained so much milky juice that it burned our mouths. Since water was very scarce, whoever ate them became very thirsty. Finally we grew so hungry that we purchased two dogs in exchange for nets and other things and a hide that I used to cover myself.

I have said already that we went naked in that land, and not being accustomed to it, we shed our skin twice a year, like snakes. Exposure to the sun and air covered our chests and backs with great sores that made it very painful to carry big and heavy loads, the ropes of which cut into the flesh on our arms.

The country is so rough and overgrown that often after we had gathered firewood in the forest and dragged it out, we would bleed freely from the thorns and spines that cut and slashed us wherever they touched us. Sometimes it happened that I was unable to carry or drag out the firewood after I had gathered it with great loss of blood. In all that trouble my only relief or consolation was to remember the passion of our Savior, Jesus Christ, and the blood he shed for me, and to consider how much greater his sufferings had been from those thorns than I from the ones I was then enduring.

I made a contract with the Indians to make combs, arrows, bows, and nets for them. We also made the matting from which their lodges are constructed and which they greatly need, for, although they know how to make it, they do not like to do any work, in order to be able to go in search of food. Whenever they work they suffer greatly from hunger.

At other times, they would make me scrape skins and tan them, and the greatest luxury I enjoyed was on the day they would give me a skin to scrape, because I scraped it very deeply in order to eat the parings, which would last me two or three days. It also happened that, while we were with these Indians and those mentioned before, we would eat a piece of meat they gave us raw, because if we broiled it the first Indian who came along would snatch it away and eat it. It seemed useless to take any pains, in view of what we might expect, nor did we care to go to any trouble in order to have it broiled and might just as well eat it raw. Such was the life we led there, and we had to earn even that scant sustenance by bartering the objects we made with our own hands.

CHAPTER TWENTY-THREE

How We Departed After Eating the Dogs

AFTER WE HAD EATEN THE DOGS it seemed to us that we had enough strength to go further on, so we commended ourselves to the guidance of God, our Lord, and took leave of these Indians, who put us on the trail of others of their language who were nearby. While on our way it began to rain and we spent the whole day walking in the wet. In addition, we lost the trail and found ourselves in a big forest, where we gathered plenty of prickly pear leaves, which we roasted that same night in an oven we made. We heated them so much that in the morning they were fit to eat. After eating them we commended ourselves to God again and left, finding the trail we had lost.

Once out of the forest, we came upon other Indian dwellings, where we saw two women and some boys, who were so frightened at the sight of us that they fled to the forest to call the men who were there. When they came they hid behind trees to look at us. We called them and they approached, though they were very afraid. After we addressed them they told us that they were very hungry, that nearby were many of their own lodges, and that they would take us to them, so that night we reached a site where there were fifty dwellings. Upon seeing us the people were astonished and showed a great deal of fear. After they had approached, they put their hands to our faces and bodies and then to their own faces and bodies. We stayed there that night, and in the morning they brought us their sick people, begging us to make the sign of the cross over them. They gave us some of what they had to eat, which were prickly pear leaves and roasted green prickly pears.

Because they treated us well and gave us everything they had, being content to be without anything for our sake, we stayed with them for several days. During that time others came from further on. When they were about to leave we told the first ones that we intended to accompany the others. This made them very sad and on their knees they begged us not to go. In the end, we took our leave. Our departure pained them greatly, and we left them in tears.

CHAPTER TWENTY-FOUR

The Customs of the Indians of That Land

FROM THE ISLE OF MISFORTUNE TO THAT LAND, all the Indians we met had the custom of not sleeping with their wives from the first sign of pregnancy until the child was two years old. Children are nursed until they are twelve years old, when they are old enough to gather their own food. We asked them why they brought their children up in that way and they replied that it was because of the great scarcity of food all over the country, since it was common, as we have noted, to go without it for two or three days, or even four. For that reason they let the little ones nurse so that in lean times they will not die. Even if they do survive, they will be very delicate and weak. When one falls ill he is left to die in the field unless he is somebody's child. Other invalids, if unable to travel, are abandoned, but a son or brother is taken along.

There is also a custom for husbands to leave their wives if they do not get along, and to remarry whomever they please. This applies to young men, but after they have had children, they stay with their wives and do not leave them.

When in any village they quarrel among themselves, they strike and beat each other until they are worn out, and only then do they separate. Sometimes their women step in and separate them, but men never interfere in these brawls. Nor do they ever use bow and arrow. After they have fought and settled the question, they take their lodges and women and go out into the countryside to live apart from the others till their anger is over. When they are no longer angry and their resentment has passed they return to the village and are friendly again, as if nothing had happened. There is no need of mediation. When a quarrel takes place between unmarried people they go to some of their neighbors, who, even if they are enemies, will welcome them with great festivity and gifts from among

66

their possessions, so that, when pacified, they return to their village wealthy.

They are all warlike and are so astute in guarding themselves from an enemy that it seems as if they had trained in Italy and in continuous warfare.[62] When they are in places where their enemies may do them harm, they set their lodges on the edge of the roughest and densest timber they can find and dig a trench close by in which they sleep. The warriors are hidden by brushwood, which has loopholes, and are so well covered and concealed that even at close range they cannot be seen.

They open a very narrow trail to the densest part of the forest and arrange a sleeping place for their women and children there. As night sets in they build fires in the lodges, so that if there should be spies about, they will think that people are inside. Before sunrise they relight the fires. If perchance someone approaches the lodges, the warriors emerge from the trenches, without being seen or discovered, and are able to inflict a great deal of damage.

In case there are no forests in which they can hide and prepare their ambushes, they settle on the plain wherever it appears most appropriate and surround the place with trenches protected by brushwood. They open loopholes in them through which their arrows can reach the enemy and they build parapets for the nighttime. Once, while I was with the Aguenes, when they were not on their guard, their enemies surprised them at midnight, killing three and wounding a number, so they fled from their houses to the forest. However, as soon as they noticed that the other Indians had gone they went back, picked up all the arrows the others had spent, and followed them, as stealthily as possible. That night they reached the others' dwellings unnoticed. Just before sunrise they attacked, killing five and wounding a great many. The rest made their escape, leaving their homes and bows behind with all their other belongings.

A short time after this the Quevenes women came, held a conversation, and made them friends again. But sometimes women are the cause of war. All these people, when they have private quarrels and are not of one family, kill each other in a treacherous way and deal most cruelly with one another.

CHAPTER TWENTY-FIVE

How Ready the Indians Are with Weapons

THESE INDIANS ARE THE READIEST PEOPLE with their weapons of any I have seen in the world. When they fear an enemy's approach they lie awake all night with their bows and a dozen arrows within reach. Before one goes to sleep he tries his bow and, should the string not be to his liking, he arranges it to suit him. Often they crawl out of their dwellings so as not to be seen and look around in every direction. If they detect anything, in less than no time they are all out in the field with their bows and arrows. Thus they remain until daybreak, running hither and thither whenever they see danger or suspect their enemies might approach. At daybreak, they unstring their bows until the time comes for them to go out to hunt.

Their bowstrings are made of deer sinews. They fight in a crouch, and while shooting at each other they talk and dart from side to side to dodge their foe's arrows. Because of this our crossbows and harquebuses will do them little damage. On the contrary, the Indians laugh at those weapons, because they present no danger to them on the plains over which they roam. They are only good in narrow areas and in swamps. Horses are what the Indians dread most, and the means by which they will be overcome.

Whoever has to fight Indians must take great care not to let them think he is disheartened or that he covets what they own. In war they must be treated very harshly, for should they notice either fear or greed, as a people they know how to bide their time waiting for revenge and take courage from their enemies' fears. After using up all their arrows, they part, each going his own way, without attempting pursuit, although one side might have more men than the other. Such is their custom.

Many times they are shot all over their bodies with arrows, but they do not die from the wounds as long as their bowels or heart is not affected. On the contrary, they recover quickly. Their eyesight, hearing, and senses in general are better, I believe, than those of any other men on earth. They can stand, and they have to stand, severe hunger, thirst, and cold, and are more accustomed and used to it than others. I wished to state this here, since, apart from the curiosity all men have about the habits and devices of others, those who might come in contact with those people should be informed of their customs and deeds, which will be of no small profit to them.

CHAPTER TWENTY-SIX

On Nations and Languages

I ALSO DO WISH TO TELL of the nations and languages encountered from the Island of Misfortune to the most recent ones, the Cuchendados. On the Isle of Misfortune two languages are spoken, one they call Cavoques, the other Han. On the mainland, facing the island, there are others, called Charruco Indians, who take their name from the woods in which they live. Further on, along the seashore, there are others who call themselves Deguenes, and across from them still others named the Mendicans. Further on, on the coast, are the Quevenes, and further inland the Marianes. Following the coast we come to the Guaycones, and in front of them inland the Yguaces. After those come the Atayos, and behind them others, called Decubadaos, of whom there are a great many further on in this direction. On the coast live the Quitoles, and in front of them, inland, the Chavavares. These are joined by the Maliacones and the Cultalchulches and others called Susolas and Comos. Ahead on the coast are the Camolas, and further on those whom we call the People of the Figs.[63]

All of them have houses and villages and speak different languages. Among them is a language in which when they call men to look at something they say "arraca" and for dogs they say "xó."

Throughout the country, they get inebriated by using a certain smoke, and will give everything they have in order to get it. They also drink something that they extract from leaves of a tree similar to a water-oak, toasting them on the fire in a container like a low-necked bottle. When the leaves are toasted they fill the container with water and hold it over the fire for long enough for the water to boil twice. Then they pour the liquid into a bowl made of a gourd cut in half. When there is a lot of foam on it they drink it as hot as they can stand, and from the time they take it out of the first vessel until they drink they shout, "Who wants to drink?" When women hear this they stand still, and although they may be carrying a very heavy load they do not dare to move. Should one of them stir, she is dishonored and beaten. In a great rage they spill the liquid they have prepared and spit up what they drank, easily and without pain. The reason for this custom, they say, is that when they want to drink that water and the women stir from the spot where they first hear the shouts, an evil substance gets into the liquid that penetrates their bodies, causing them to die before long. All the time the water boils the vessel must be kept covered. Should it be uncovered while a woman comes along they pour it out and do not drink it. It is yellow and they drink it for three days without partaking of any food, each consuming an *arroba*[64] and a half every day.

When the women have their cycle they seek food only for themselves, because nobody else will eat what they bring.

During the time I was among them I saw something very repulsive, namely, a man married to another. These are impotent and womanish beings who dress like and do the work of women. They carry heavy loads but do not use a bow. Among these Indians we saw many of them. They are more robust than other men, taller, and can bear heavy loads.

CHAPTER TWENTY-SEVEN

How We Moved and Were Received

AFTER PARTING FROM THE INDIANS we had left in tears, we went with the others to their homes and were very warmly received. They brought us their children to touch and gave us a great deal of mesquite flour. The mesquite is a fruit, which, while on the tree, is very bitter, like the carob bean. It is eaten with earth and then becomes sweet and very palatable. The way they prepare it is to dig a hole in the ground to a depth that suits them, and after the fruit is put in the hole, they pound it to a meal with a piece of wood the thickness of a leg and one and a half arm lengths long. They add several handfuls to the earth that mixes with it in the hole and then pound it until it is very fine. After that they empty it into a container like a small, round basket, and pour in enough water to cover it fully, so that there is water on top. Then the one who has done the pounding tastes it, and if it appears not sweet enough to him he calls for more earth to be added. He does this until it suits his taste. Then they all squat around and everyone reaches out with his hand and takes as much as he can. They set the seeds and peelings apart on hides, and then the one who has done the pounding throws them back into the basket, pouring water over them again. They squeeze out the juice and water, and they again put husks and seeds on hides, at every pounding repeating the operation three or four times. Those who take part in that banquet, which for them is a great occasion, get very big bellies from the earth and water they swallow.

The Indians made a great feast of this in our behalf, and danced and celebrated all the time we were with them. At night six Indians kept watch at the entrance to each lodge in which one of us slept, without allowing anybody to enter before sunrise.

When we were about to leave a few women from the Indians living further on arrived and, finding out the location of their homes, we left, although the Indians entreated us to remain a day longer, since our destination was very far away and there was no trail to it. They pointed out how tired the women who had just arrived were, but that if they rested until the next day, they could accompany and guide us. We left, nevertheless, and soon the women followed with others of the village.

There being no trails in that country, we soon lost our way. At the end of four leagues we reached a spring where we met the women who had followed us, and who told us of all the trouble they had had to find us. We went on, taking them with us as guides.

In the afternoon we crossed a big river with water up to our chests, which had a swift current and was perhaps as wide as the river in Seville.[65] At sunset we reached a hundred Indian huts and, as we approached, the people came out to welcome us, slapping their thighs and shouting frightfully. They carried gourds into which they had bored holes, which they then filled with pebbles, which are ceremonial objects of great importance. They only use them at dances or to perform cures, and other than them nobody dares to touch them. They claim that the gourds have healing powers and that they come from Heaven, since they are not found in that country. Nor do they know where the gourds come from, only that the rivers carry them downstream when they rise and flood the land.

Their excitement and eagerness to touch us was so great that, everyone wanting to be first, they nearly squeezed us to death. They carried us to their homes without allowing our feet to touch the ground. So many people crowded in on us that we took refuge in the lodges they had prepared for our accommodation and in no manner consented to be feted by them on that night.

They spent the whole night in celebration and dancing, and the next morning they brought every living soul of the village to be touched by us and to have the cross made over them, as we had done with the others Indians with whom we had been.[66] Then they gave a great many arrows to the women of the other village who had come with theirs. The next day when we went on all the people of that village went with us, and when we came to other Indians we were as well received as anywhere in the past; they also gave us their possessions and the deer they had killed during the day. Among these we saw a new custom. Those who were with us took the bows, arrows, shoes, and beads, if they wore any, from the people who came to get cured and placed them before us to induce us to cure the sick. As soon as they had been treated they went away contented, saying they felt well.

We left there as well and went to other Indians, by whom we were also very well received. They brought us their sick who, after we had made the sign of the cross over them, said they were healed, and the one who did not get well still believed we might cure him. They all rejoiced at what those we had treated told them and danced so much that they would not let us sleep.

CHAPTER TWENTY-EIGHT

On Another New Custom

AFTER WE LEFT THOSE INDIANS we went to many other lodges, but from there on a new custom began. While we were welcomed everywhere, those who came with us treated those who received us badly, taking away their homes and belongings without leaving them anything. It saddened us to see how those who were so good to us were abused. Besides, we were afraid that this behavior might cause trouble and strife, but we could not dare to interfere or punish the transgressors, and had to wait until we had more authority over them. Furthermore, the sufferers themselves, when they noticed how badly we felt, consoled us by telling us not to worry; that they were happy to see their homes so well employed, and that, besides, further on they would repay themselves from other Indians, who were very rich. During the whole journey we were very worried by the number of people following us. We could not escape them, although we tried, because they were so anxious to touch us. They were so obtrusive that in three hours we could not be done with them. The following day they brought us all the people of the village; most of them had one cloudy eye, while others were totally blind from the same cause, which amazed us. They were well built, of very good physique, and whiter than any we had met until then.

There we began to see mountains, and it seemed as if they swept down from the direction of the North Sea,[67] and so, from what the Indians told us, we believe they are fifteen leagues from the ocean. From there we went with the Indians toward the aforesaid mountains and they took us to some of their relatives. They did not want to lead us anywhere but to their own people in order to prevent their enemies from having any share in the great boon that, it seemed to them, it was to see us. And as soon as we arrived those with us would sack the houses of the others; but as the latter knew of the custom before our coming, they hid some of their chattels, and, after welcoming us with a great deal of rejoicing, they took out the things they had concealed and presented them to us, beads and ocher, and several little bags of silver.[68] We, following the custom, immediately turned the gifts over to the Indians who had come in our company, and after they had given us these presents they began their dances and celebrations, and sent for others from another nearby village to come and look at us. In the afternoon they all came and brought us beads, bows, and other little things, which we also distributed.

The next day, as we were going to leave, they all wanted to take us to other friends of theirs, who dwelt on a spur of the mountains. They said there were a great many lodges and people who would give us many things, but, since it was out of our way, we did not want to go there, and continued on the plain, though near the mountains, thinking that they were not far from the coast. All the people there are very bad, and we preferred to cross the country-side, since further inland they were in better condition and treated us better. We also felt sure that we would find the country more thickly settled and with more resources. In the end, we did this because, in crossing the country, we would see much more of its particulars, so that, in case God our Lord should be pleased to spare one of us and take him back to a land of Christians, he might give an account of it.

When the Indians saw we were determined not to go where they wanted, they said that nobody lived where we intended to go, nor were there prickly pears or any other food, and they entreated us to wait one day longer with them, to which we consented. Two Indians were sent out to look for people on our proposed route.

We departed on the following day, taking many of them along. The women carried water, and our authority had become so great that no one dared to drink without our permission. After going two leagues we met the men who had been sent out in search of people, but who had not found any. The Indians seemed to be saddened by this and again begged us to take the mountain trail, but we persisted. Seeing this, they took a mournful leave of us and turned back downriver to their homes, while we proceeded upstream.

Soon we met two women carrying loads. When they saw us they stopped, put down their loads, and brought us some of what they contained, which was cornmeal. They told us that further upstream we would come upon dwellings, plenty of prickly pears, and some of the same meal. We left them there, since they were going to those from whom we had just taken leave, and we walked on until at sunset we reached a village of about twenty lodges, where we were welcomed with tears and deep sorrow. They already knew that, wherever we arrived, the people would be robbed and plundered by those in our company. Seeing us alone, they lost their fear, and gave us prickly pears, though nothing else. We stayed there overnight.

At daybreak the same Indians we had left the day before surprised the lodges. Since the people had thought they were safe, they were unprepared and had had neither time nor place to hide anything. They were stripped of all their chattels, at which they wept bitterly. In consolation, the robbers told them that we were children of the sun and had the power to cure the sick or kill them. They told other lies, even bigger ones than those they invent to suit their own purposes. They also enjoined them to treat us with great reverence, be careful not to arouse our wrath, to give us all their possessions, and to guide us to where there were many people, and that wherever we should come to they should steal and rob everything the others had, which was the custom.

CHAPTER TWENTY-NINE

How They Steal from One Another

AFTER GIVING THESE INSTRUCTIONS and teaching the people how to behave, they went back and left us with these Indians, who, mindful of what the others had said, began to treat us with the same respect and awe. We traveled in their company for three days. They took us to where there were many Indians, and went ahead to tell them of our coming, repeating what they had heard as well as adding to it, for all these Indians are great gossipers and liars, particularly when they think it will be to their benefit. As we neared the lodges all the inhabitants came out to welcome us, with great rejoicing and show, and, among other things, two of their medicine men gave us gourds. From there onward we carried gourds, which greatly added to our authority since they hold these ceremonial objects in high regard. Our companions sacked the dwellings, but since there were many houses and they only few in number, they could not carry away all they took, so that more than half was left to waste. Thence we turned inland for more than fifty leagues, following the slopes of the mountains, and at the end of them came upon forty dwellings.

There, among the other things they gave us, Andrés Dorantes got a large copper rattle on which a face was represented, which they held in great esteem. They said it had been obtained from some of their neighbors. Upon asking them whence it had come, they claimed to have brought it from the north, where there was much of it and it was highly prized. We understood that wherever it might have come from there must be foundries and that metal was cast in molds. Leaving on the following day, we crossed a ridge seven leagues long whose stones were composed of iron slag. At night we came to many dwellings, situated on the banks of a very beautiful river.

The men from these dwellings came out to greet us halfway, with their children on their backs. They gave us a number of pouches of silver and powdered antimony, with which they paint their faces, and many beads and cow-skin robes, and loaded those who came with us with all their chattels. These people ate prickly pears and pine nuts; in that country there are small, sweet-pine trees[69] the cones of which are like small eggs, but the nuts of which are better than those of Castile, because the husks are thin. When the nuts are still green they grind them and make little balls out of them, which they eat. When dried they grind the nuts with the husks and eat them as meal. Those who had welcomed us, when they had touched our bodies, returned to their houses on a run. Then they came back again, and never stopped running back and forth. In this way they brought us a great many things for our journey.

Here they brought me a man who a long time ago, they said, had been shot through the right side of the back with an arrow, the head of which stuck close to his heart. He said it caused a great deal of pain and because of it he was always sick. I touched that area of his body and felt the arrowhead, which had pierced the cartilage. I cut open his breast with a knife as far as the spot. The arrow point had gotten athwart, and was very difficult to remove. By cutting deeper and inserting the point of the knife, with great effort I removed it. It was very long. Then, with a deer bone, according to my knowledge of surgery, I made two stitches. After I had extracted the arrow they begged me for it and I gave it to them. The whole village came to look at it. They sent it further inland so that the people there might see it as well, and on account of all this they held many dances and festivities, as they often do. The next day I cut the stitches, and the Indian was well.[70] He said that he did not feel the least pain.

Among these Indians, all over the country, this cure gave us as much fame as they were capable of conceiving and respecting. We showed them our rattle, and they told us that where it had come from there were a great many sheets of the same metal buried, that it was something they valued highly, and that there were permanent dwellings there. We believe it is near the South Sea, for we always heard that that sea was richer than that of the north.

After leaving these people we traveled among so many different tribes and languages that nobody's memory can recall them all. They always robbed each other, but those who lost and those who gained were equally content. The number of our companions became so large that we could no longer control them.

Throughout these valleys each Indian carried a club three palms in length. They all moved in a row, and whenever one of the many hares that live there jumped out they would close in upon the game and rain so many blows upon it that it was amazing to see. In this way they drove the hare from one to the other and, to my mind, it was the most agreeable chase that one could imagine, for many a time they would come right to one's hands. When we camped at night they gave us so many that each of us had eight or ten.[71] The Indians who carried bows would not take part in this, but went to the mountains after deer, and when at night they came back it was with five or six deer for each of us, with birds, quail, and other game. In short, everything these people could kill they set before us, without ever daring to touch anything, even if they were dying of hunger, unless we blessed it first. This was their custom from the time they joined us.

The women brought many mats, with which they built us houses, one for each of us and for those people attached to him. After this we would order them to broil the deer and hares, everything they had taken, which they quickly did, in ovens they built for that purpose. We partook a little of everything, giving the rest to the principal man among those who had come with us for distribution to everyone. Everyone then came with the share he had received for us to breathe on it and bless it, or they would not dare to eat it. Often we had with us three to four thousand people and it was very tiresome to have to breathe on and make the sign of the cross over every morsel they ate or drank. They would come to ask our permission for many other things they wanted to do, so it is easy to understand how much we were inconvenienced. The women brought us prickly pears, spiders, worms, and whatever else they could find, for they would rather starve than partake of anything that had not first passed through our hands.

While traveling with them, we crossed a big river that came from the north and, crossing about thirty leagues of plains, met a number of people that came from afar to meet us on the trail, who treated us like the earlier ones.

CHAPTER THIRTY

How the Manner of Reception Changed

FROM HERE ON there was a change in the manner of reception, insofar as those who would meet us on the trail with gifts were no longer robbed by the Indians of our company, but after we had entered their homes they tendered us all they possessed, including their dwellings. We turned over everything to the principals for distribution. Invariably those who had been deprived of their belongings would follow us, in order to repair their losses, so that our retinue became very large. They would tell them to be careful and not conceal anything of what they owned, since it could not be done without our knowledge, and then we would cause their death. This frightened them so much that on the first few days after joining us they would tremble all the time, and would not dare to speak or lift their eyes to Heaven.

They guided us for more than fifty leagues through a desert of very rugged mountains, so arid that there was no game. Consequently, we experienced a great deal of hunger. Finally we forded a very big river, with its water reaching to our chests. From then on many of our people began to show the effects of the hunger and hardships they had undergone in those mountains, which were extremely barren and difficult to travel in.

The same Indians led us to a plain beyond the chain of mountains, where people from far away came to meet us. They treated us in the same manner as before, and they gave so many presents to the Indians who came with us that, unable to carry it all, they left half of it. We told the givers to take it back, so they would not lose it, but they refused, saying it was not their custom to take back what they had once offered, so it was left to waste. We told these people that our route was toward the sunset and they replied that in that direction people lived very far away. So we ordered them to send there and inform the inhabitants that we were coming. They begged to be excused from this task, because the others were their enemies and they did not want us to go to them. In the end they did not dare to disobey, and sent two women, one of their own and the other a captive. They selected women because these can trade everywhere, even if there is war.

We followed the women to a place where it had been agreed we should wait for them. After five days they had not returned, and the Indians explained that it might be because they had not found anybody. So we told them to take us north, and they repeated that there were no people, except very far away, and neither food nor water. Nevertheless we insisted, saying that we wanted to go there, and they still excused themselves as best they could, until at last we became angry.

One night I went away to sleep out in the field apart from them, but they soon came to where I was and remained awake all night greatly alarmed, talking to me, saying how frightened they were. They entreated us not to be angry any longer, because, even if it meant their death, they would take us where we chose. We continued to feign anger in order to keep them in suspense, until a singular thing happened.

On that day many of them fell ill, and on the following day eight of them died. All over the country where it was known, they became so afraid that it seemed as if the mere sight of us would kill them. They besought us not to be angry, nor to will the death of any more of their number, for they were convinced that we killed them by merely wishing it. In truth, we were very much concerned about it, for seeing this great mortality, we dreaded that all of them might die or desert us in their terror, while those further on, upon learning of it, would avoid us. We prayed to God our Lord to assist us and the sick began to get well.

Then we saw something that astonished us very much. While the parents, brothers, and wives of the dead had shown deep grief at their illness, from the moment they died the survivors made no demonstration whatsoever, neither weeping nor even talking with one another, nor did they dare to go near the bodies until we ordered their burial.

In the more than fifteen days we remained with them we never saw them talk together, not even the laughing or crying of a child. Once, a child began to cry and was carried off some distance where, with some very sharp mice-teeth, they scratched it from the shoulders to almost the entire length of its legs. Angered by this act of cruelty, I took them to task for it, and they said it was done to punish the child for having wept in my presence. Their apprehensions caused the others who came to see us to give us what they owned, since they knew that we did not take anything for ourselves, but left it all to the Indians. They were the most docile people we met in the country, of the best makeup, and on the whole of good physique.

The sick had recovered, and when we had already been there three days, the women we had sent out returned, saying that they had met very few people, nearly all having gone after the cows, since it was the season. So we ordered those who had been sick to remain and those who were well to accompany us, and that the same women should go with us and two days' travel from there get people to come to meet us on the trail to receive us.

The next morning all those who were strong enough came along, and at the end of the three-day journey we halted. Alonso del Castillo and Estevanico, the Negro, left with the women as guides, and the captive woman took them to the river that flows between the mountains, where there was a village in which her father lived. These were the first dwellings we saw that were like real houses. Castillo and Estevanico went there and, after holding a conversation with the Indians, at the end of three days Castillo returned to where he had left us, bringing with him five or six of the Indians. He told us how he had found permanent houses that were inhabited, the people of which ate beans and squash, and that he had also seen corn.

Of all things on earth this gave us the greatest pleasure, and we gave endless thanks to our Lord for this news. Castillo also said that the Negro was coming to meet us on the way, nearby, with all the people of the houses. For that reason we started out and after going a league and a half met the Negro and the people that came to welcome us, who gave us beans and many squashes to eat, gourds to carry water in, cowhide robes, and other things. Since those people and the Indians of our company were enemies, and did not understand each other, we took leave of the latter, leaving them all that had been given to us, while we went on with the former and, six leagues beyond, when night was already approaching, reached their houses, where they received us with great celebration. Here we remained one day, and left on the next, taking them with us to other permanent houses, where they subsisted on the same food as well.

From there on we encountered a new custom. The people who heard of our approach did not, as before, come out to meet us on the way, but we found them at their homes, and they had other houses ready for us. They were all seated with their faces turned to the wall, their heads bowed and their hair pulled over their eyes. Their belongings had been gathered in a heap in the middle of the floor. From there on they began to give us many robes made of skins. There was nothing they would not give us. They are the best-formed people we have seen, the liveliest and most capable, who best understood us and answered our questions. We called them the Indians of the Cow, because most of the cows die near there, and because they go more than fifty leagues upstream to kill many of them. They go completely naked, just like the first Indians we met. The women and some men are covered with deerskins, especially the old ones, who are of no use anymore in war.

The country is well settled. We asked them why they did not raise corn, and they replied that they were afraid of losing the crops, since for two successive years it had not rained, and the seasons were so dry that the moles had eaten it, so that they did not dare to plant any more until it had rained very hard. They also begged us to ask Heaven for rain, which we promised to do. We also wanted to know from where they brought their corn, and they said it came from where the sun sets, and that it was found all over the country, and the shortest way to it was in that direction. We asked them to tell us how to go, since they did not want to go themselves, and to tell us about the route.

They said we should travel upriver toward the north, on which trail we would not find a thing to eat for seventeen days, except a fruit called *chacan*, which they grind between stones, but even then it cannot be eaten, because it is so coarse and dry. This was indeed so, since they showed it to us and we could not eat it. They also said that, all the time we would be going upstream, we would be traveling among people who were their enemies, although they spoke the same language. They would not be able to give us food, but would receive us very willingly, and give us many cotton blankets, hides, and other things; but it seemed to them that we ought not to take that route.

In doubt as to what should be done and which was the best and most advantageous path to take, we remained with them for two days. They gave us beans and squash. Their way of cooking them is so new and strange that I want to describe it here in order to show how different and queer the devices and industries of human beings are. They have no pots. In order to cook their food they fill a medium-sized gourd with water and place stones that are easily heated into a fire. When they are hot to the point of scorching they take them out with wooden tongs, and thrust them into the water in the gourd, until it boils. As soon as it boils they put what they want to cook into it, always taking out the stones as they cool off and throwing in hot ones to keep the water boiling steadily in order to cook whatever they wish.

CHAPTER THIRTY-ONE

How We Followed the Corn Trail

AFTER TWO DAYS, we decided to go in search of corn and not to follow the road to the cows, since the latter carried us to the north, which meant a very great circuit, and since we were always sure that by going toward sunset we should reach our desired goal.

So we went on our way and crossed the whole country to the South Sea. Our resolution was not shaken by a great fear of hunger, which the Indians said we should suffer, and we did indeed suffer during our first seventeen days of travel. All along the river, and in the course of these seventeen days, we received plenty of cowhides, and did not eat their famous fruit. Our food for each day consisted of a handful of deer tallow, which we always sought to hold onto for that purpose. So we endured these seventeen days, at the end of which we crossed the river and marched for seventeen days more toward the sunset through the plains between two mountain ranges. At sunset, on a plain between very high mountains, we met people who, for one third of the year, eat nothing but powdered straw, and since we passed by just at that time, we had to eat it as well, until, at the end of that journey we found some permanent houses with plenty of harvested corn, the meal of which they gave us in great quantities, as well as squash, beans, and cotton blankets, all of which we loaded onto those who had conducted us there, so that they went home the most contented people on earth. We gave God our Lord many thanks for having taken us where there was plenty to eat.

Among the houses there were several made of earth, and others of cane matting. From here we traveled more than a hundred leagues, always coming upon permanent houses and a great stock of corn and beans, and they gave us many deer hides and cotton blankets better than those of New Spain. They also gave us plenty of beads made of the coral found in the South Sea and good turquoises, which they get from the north. In the end, they gave us everything they owned. They presented Dorantes with five emeralds shaped like arrow points, the arrows of which they use in their feasts and dances. Because they seemed to be of very good quality, I asked where they got them, and they said they came from some very high mountains toward the north, where they traded feather brushes and parrot plumes for them. They also said that there were villages with many people and big houses there.

Among these people we found the women better treated than in any other part of the Indies as far as we have seen. They wear cotton shirts that reach down to the knee and over them half-sleeves of scraped deerskin, with strips that hang down to the ground, which they clean with certain roots that clean very well and keep them tidy. The shirts are open in front and tied with strings. They wear shoes.

They all came to us so we might touch and make the sign of the cross over them. They were so obtrusive that they made it difficult to endure since everyone, sick and healthy, wanted to be blessed. It happened frequently that women of our company would give birth to children and immediately bring them to have the sign of the cross made over them and have us touch the babes. They always accompanied us until we were again in the care of others. Among all these people it was believed that we came from Heaven. What they do not understand or is new to them they are wont to say comes from above.

While traveling with them we used to go the whole day without food, until nighttime, and then we would eat so little that the Indians were amazed. They never saw us tired, because we were, in reality, so inured to hardships that we no longer felt them. We exercised great authority over them, and carried ourselves with gravity so that, in order to maintain it, we said very little to them. We had the Negro talk to them all the time; he inquired about the road we should follow, the villages—in short, about everything we wished to know. We came across a great variety and number of languages, and God our Lord favored us with a knowledge of all of it, because they always could understand us and we them. When we asked they would answer by signs, as if they spoke our tongue and we theirs for, although we spoke six languages, we could not use them everywhere, since we encountered more than a thousand different ones.

In that part of the country, in order to meet us and bring us all they possessed, those at war would immediately make peace and become friendly to each other. We left the whole country in this way.

We told them by signs that they understood, that in Heaven there was a man we called God, who had created Heaven and earth, and whom we worshipped as our Lord; that we did as he ordered us to do, since all good things came from his hand, and that if they were to do the same it would go very well with them. They were so well inclined that, had there been a language in which we could have made ourselves perfectly understood, we would have left them all Christians. All this we gave them to understand as clearly as possible. Afterward, when the sun rose, with great shouts they would lift their clasped hands to Heaven and then pass them all over their bodies. They did the same thing at sunset. These people are well made and are apt to follow any line that is well traced for them.

CHAPTER THIRTY-TWO

How They Gave Us Hearts of Deer

IN THE VILLAGE where they had given us emeralds, they also gave Dorantes more than six hundred open hearts of deer, of which they always kept a great supply for eating. For this reason we gave their settlement the name of "village of the hearts."[72] The pass through it leads into many provinces near the South Sea, and any one who should attempt to get there by another route must surely be lost, since there is no corn on the coast. They eat powdered fox-tail grass, straw, and fish, which they catch in the sea on rafts, for they have no canoes. The women cover their loins with straw and grass. They are a very shy and sad people.

We believe that, near the coast, in line with the villages we followed, there are more than a thousand leagues of inhabited land, where they have plenty of victuals, since they raise three crops of beans and corn a year. There are three kinds of deer, one as large as Castilian calves. They live in huts. They have a poison taken from certain trees the size of our apple trees. They need but pick the fruit and rub their arrows with it; and if there is no fruit they gather a branch and do the same with its milky sap. Many of those trees are so poisonous that if the leaves are pounded and washed in water near by, a deer or any other animal that drinks it will burst at once. We stayed in this village for three days, and at a day's journey from it was another, where a rainstorm overtook us and the river rose so high that we could not cross it and had to remain there for fifteen days.

During this time Castillo saw, on the neck of an Indian, a little buckle from a sword belt, and in it was sewed a horseshoe nail. He took it from the Indian and we asked what it was; they said it had come from Heaven. We further asked who had brought it, and they answered that some men, with beards like ours, had come from Heaven to that river; that they had horses, lances, and swords, and had lanced two of them.

As cautiously as possible, we then inquired what had become of those men; and they replied that they had gone to sea, putting their lances into the water and then going into it themselves, and that afterward they saw them on top of the waves moving toward sunset.

We gave God our Lord many thanks for what we had heard, for we were despairing of ever hearing of Christians again. On the other hand, we were sad and dejected, lest those people had come by sea for the sake of discovery only.[73] Finally, having such positive notice of them, we hastened onward, always finding more traces of the Christians and told the Indians that we were now sure to find the Christians and would tell them not to kill Indians or make slaves of them nor take them away from their homelands, or do any other harm, which made them very happy.

We traveled over a great part of the country and found it all deserted, since the people had fled to the mountains, leaving their houses and fields out of fear of the Christians. This filled our hearts with sorrow, seeing the land so fertile and beautiful, so full of water and streams, but abandoned and the places burned down, and the people, so thin and wan, fleeing and hiding. Because they did not raise any crops their destitution had become so great that they ate tree bark and roots. We had our share of this hunger all the way along, because in their indigence they could provide little for us and it looked as if they were going to die. They brought us blankets, which they had been concealing from the Christians, and gave them to us, and told us how the Christians had come into the country before and had destroyed and burned the villages, taking with them half the men and all the women and children, and how those who could escaped by running off. Seeing them in this plight, afraid to stay anywhere and that they neither would nor could cultivate the soil, preferring to die rather than suffer such cruelties, while they showed the greatest pleasure at being with us, we began to understand that the Indians who were in arms against the Christians might treat us badly in retaliation for what the Christians did to them. But when it pleased God our Lord to take us to those Indians, they respected us and held us to be precious, as the former ones had done, and even a little more so. This astonished us somewhat, while it clearly shows how, in order to bring those people to Christianity and obedience unto Your Imperial Majesty, they should be well treated, and not otherwise.

They took us to a village on the crest of a mountain, which can be reached only by a very steep trail, where we found a great many people who had gathered there out of dread of the Christians. They received us very well, giving us all they had: more than two thousand loads of corn, which we distributed among the poor, famished people who had led us to the place. The next day we dispatched, as we were wont to do, four runners, to call together in a village three days' journey away as many people as could be reached. On the next day we followed with all the people we had there, always meeting with signs and vestiges of where the Christians had slept.

At noon we met our messengers, who told us they had not found anybody, because they were all hidden in the woods lest the Christians kill or enslave them. On the previous night they had seen the Christians and watched their movements, under cover of some trees behind which they concealed themselves, and saw the Christians take many Indians along in chains. The people who were with us became frightened at this and some turned back to give the alarm through the land that Christians were coming. Many more would have done the same had we not told them to stay and have no fear, which quieted them down and comforted them. We had Indians with us at the time who came from a distance of a hundred leagues, and whom we could not induce to go back to their homes. So, in order to reassure them, we slept there that night, and the next day went further, and slept on the road. The day after, those we had sent to explore guided us to where they had seen the Christians. Reaching the place at the hour of vespers, we clearly saw they had told the truth and that judging from the stakes to which the horses had been tied, there were horsemen among them.

From here, which is called the Pututan River,[74] to the river which Diego de Guzman reached, there may be, from the place where we first heard of the Christians, eighty leagues; then to the village where the rain overtook us, twelve leagues; from there to the Village of the Hearts five leagues; and from there to the South Sea twelve leagues. Throughout all that country, wherever it is mountainous, we saw many signs of gold, antimony, iron, copper, and other metals. Where the permanent houses are it is so hot that even in January the air is very warm. From there to the southward the land, which is uninhabited as far as the North Sea, is very barren and poor. We suffered great and almost incredible starvation there; and those who roam through that country and dwell in it are very cruel people, of evil inclinations and habits. The Indians who live in permanent houses and those in the rear of them pay no attention to gold or silver, nor have they any use for either of these metals.

CHAPTER THIRTY-THREE

How We Saw Traces of Christians

HAVING SEEN POSITIVE TRACES of Christians and become satisfied they were very nearby, we gave many thanks to our Lord for redeeming us from our sad and gloomy captivity. Anyone can imagine our delight when he reflects on how long we had been in that land and how many dangers and hardships we had suffered. That night I entreated one of my companions to go after the Christians, who were moving through the part of the country we had pacified and quieted and who were three days ahead of where we were. They did not like my suggestion and excused themselves from going on the grounds of being tired and worn out, although any of them might have done it far better than I, being younger and stronger.

Seeing their reluctance, in the morning I took the Negro and eleven Indians with me and, following the trail, went in search of the Christians. On that day we made ten leagues, passing three places where they had slept. The next morning I came upon four Christians on horseback who, seeing me in such strange attire and in the company of Indians, were greatly startled. They stared at me for quite a while, speechless. Their surprise was so great that they could not find words to ask me anything. I spoke first, and told them to lead me to their captain, and together we went to Diego de Alcazar, their commander.

After I had addressed him he said that he himself was in a plight, since for many days he had been unable to capture Indians, did not know where to go, and that starvation was beginning to place them in dire straits. I stated to him that, in the rear of me, at a distance of ten leagues, were Dorantes and Castillo, with many people who had guided us through the country. He at once dispatched three horsemen, with fifty of his Indians, and the Negro went with them as a guide, while I remained and asked them to give me a certified statement of the date—year, month, and day—I had met them, as well as the condition in which I had come. They complied with this request.

From this river to the village called San Miguel, which belongs to the government of New Galicia,[75] is thirty leagues.

CHAPTER THIRTY-FOUR

How I Sent for the Christians

FIVE DAYS LATER Andrés Dorantes and Alonso del Castillo came with those who had gone in quest of them. They brought along more than six hundred Indians from the village, the people whom the Christians had caused to flee to the woods and who were hiding about in the country. Those who had come with us as far as that place had taken them out of their hiding places and turned them over to the Christians. They had also dispatched the others who had come that far.

When they arrived, Alcaraz begged me to send for the people of the villages along the banks of the river who were hiding in the forests; he also asked me to order them to fetch supplies. There was no occasion for the latter, since the Indians always took good care to bring us whatever they could. Nevertheless, we sent our messengers at once to call them, and six hundred persons came with all the corn they had, in pots closed with clay, which they had buried to conceal them. They also brought nearly everything else they possessed, but we only took some of the food, giving the rest to the Christians for distribution among themselves.

Thereupon we had many and bitter quarrels with the Christians, for they wanted to make slaves of our Indians, and we grew so angry at it that at our departure we forgot to take along many bows, pouches, and arrows, as well as the five emeralds,[76] so they were left and lost to us. We gave the Christians a great many cow-skin robes and other objects, and had a great deal of trouble in persuading the Indians to return home and plant their crops in peace. They insisted on accompanying us until, according to their custom, we should be in custody of other Indians, because otherwise they were afraid to die; besides, as long as we were with them, they had no fear of the Christians and of their lances. The Christians were greatly vexed by all this and told their own interpreter to say to the Indians how we were of their own race but had gone astray for a while, and were people of no luck and little heart, whereas they were the lords of the land, whom they should obey and serve. The Indians paid little attention to all this talk. They talked among themselves, saying that the Christians lied, for we had come from sunrise, while they had come from where the sun sets; that we cured the sick, while they had killed those who were healthy; that we went naked and barefoot, whereas they wore clothes and went on horseback and carried lances. Also, we asked for nothing, but gave away all we were presented with, while they seemed to have no other aim than to steal what they could, and never gave anything to anybody. In short, they recalled all our deeds, and praised them highly, contrasting them with the conduct of the others.

They told this to the Christians' interpreter and made the others understand it by means of a language they have among them and by which we understood each other. We call those who use that language properly Primahaitu, which means the same as Bizcaya.[77] We found this language in use for more than four hundred leagues of those we traveled and the only one among them over that extent of country. In the end, we never could convince the Indians that we belonged to the other Christians and only with considerable trouble and insistence could we prevail upon them to go home.

We recommended to them to rest easy and settle again in their villages, tilling and planting their fields as usual, which, from lying waste, were overgrown, though it is beyond all doubt the best land in the Indies, the most fertile and productive of food, where they raise three crops every year. It has an abundance of fruit, very handsome rivers, and other good waters. There is evidence of gold and silver mines; the inhabitants are of good disposition and willingly attend to the Christians, that is, those of the natives that are friendly and of good will. They are much better inclined than the natives of Mexico. In short, it is a country that lacks nothing to be very beneficial. When the Indians took leave of us they said they would do as we had told them, and settle in their villages, provided the Christians would not interfere, and so I say and affirm that, if they should not do it, it will be the fault of the Christians.

After we had dispatched the Indians, under the protection of the Christians, they sent us a certain magistrate named Cebreros, who had with him three other men. This will clearly show how much the designs of men can miscarry. We went on with the idea of ensuring the Indians' freedom, but just when we believed we had achieved this, the opposite took place. In order to keep us from communicating with the Indians, he took us through forests and uninhabited country, which, in fact prevented us from seeing what the Christians were doing. They had planned to fall upon the Indians we had sent back in their imagined security and in peace, and that was the plan they carried out.

For two days they took us through forests with no trail, lost and without water, so we all expected to die from thirst. Seven of our men perished and many of the companions the Christians had taken along could not reach before noon of the following day the place where we found water that same night. We traveled with them for about twenty-five leagues and at last came to a settlement of peaceable Indians. There the magistrate left us and went ahead to a place called Culiacan, three leagues ahead, where Melchor Diaz[78] was chief magistrate and the captain of the province.

CHAPTER THIRTY-FIVE

How Well the Chief Magistrate Received Us on the Night of Our Arrival

AS SOON AS THE CHIEF MAGISTRATE was informed of our arrival, that very night he came to where we were. He was deeply moved, and praised God for having delivered us in his great pity. He spoke to us and treated us very well, tendering us, in his name, and in behalf of the governor, Nuño de Guzman, all he had and whatever he might be able to do. He seemed to be very grieved at the bad reception and poor treatment we had met at the hands of Alcaraz and the others and we truly believed that, had he been there at the time, the things done to us and the Indians would not have occurred.

We spent the night there, and were about to leave on the morning of the next day, but the chief magistrate entreated us to stay. He said that by remaining we would render a great service to God and to Your Majesty, since the country was depopulated, lying waste, and nearly destroyed and that the Indians had fled and were hiding in the woods, refusing to come out and settle again in their villages. He suggested that we send for them and urge them, in the name of God and of Your Majesty, to return to the plain and cultivate the soil again.

This struck us as difficult to put into effect. We had none of our Indians with us, nor any of those who usually accompanied us and understood such matters. At last we ventured to select two Indians from among those being held as captives there and who were from that part of the country. These had been with the Christians whom we first met, and had seen the people that came in our company and knew, through the latter, of the great power and authority we exercised all through the land, the marvels we had worked, the cures we had performed, and many other particulars. With these Indians we sent others from the village, together to call those who had taken refuge in the mountains, as well as those from the river of Petatlan, where we had first met the Christians, and tell them to come, because we wished to talk to them. In order to ensure their coming, we gave the messengers one of the large gourds we had carried, which were our chief insignia and tokens of great power.

Thus provided and instructed, they left and were absent seven days, after which they returned. With them were three chiefs of those who had been in the mountains and fifteen men. They presented us with beads, turquoises, and feathers, and the messengers said the people from the river whence we had started could not be found, since the Christians had again driven them into the wilderness.

Melchor Diaz told the interpreter to speak to the Indians in our name and say that he came in the name of God, who is in Heaven, and that we had traveled the world over nine years, telling all the people we met to believe in God and serve him, for he was the Lord of everything upon earth, who rewarded the good, whereas he meted out eternal punishment of fire to the bad. That when the good ones died he took them up to heaven, where everyone lived forever and there was neither hunger nor thirst, nor any other wants—only the greatest imaginable glory. But that those who would not believe in him nor obey his commandments he thrust into a huge fire beneath the earth and into the company of demons, where the fire never went out, but tormented them forever. Moreover, he said that if they became Christians and served God in the manner we directed, the Christians would look upon them as brethren and treat them very well, while we would command that no harm should be done to them; nor should they be taken out of their country, and the Christians would become their great friends. If they refused to do so, then the Christians would treat them badly and carry them off to another country as slaves.

To this they replied, through the interpreter, that they would be very good Christians and serve God.

Upon being asked whom they worshipped and to whom they offered sacrifices, to whom they prayed for health and water for the fields of corn, they said, to a man in Heaven. We asked what was his name, and they said Aguar, and that they believed he had created the world and everything in it.

We again asked them how they came to know this, and they said their fathers and grandfathers had told them and they had known it for a very long time, that water and all good things came from him. We explained that this being of whom they spoke was the same one we called God and that thereafter they should give him that name and worship and serve him as we commanded, when they would fare very well.

They replied that they understood us thoroughly and would do as we had said.

So we bade them come out of the mountains and be at ease, peaceable, and settle the land again, rebuilding their houses. Among these houses they should rear one to God, placing at its entrance a cross like the one we had, and when Christians came, they should go out to welcome them with crosses in their hands, in place of bows and other weapons, and take the Christians to their homes and give them something to eat from what they had. If they did so, the Christians would do them no harm, but be their friends.

They promised to do as we ordered, and the captain gave them blankets, treating them handsomely, and they went away, taking along the two captives that had acted as our messengers.

This took place in presence of a notary and of a great many witnesses.

CHAPTER THIRTY-SIX

How We Had Churches Built in That Land

AS SOON AS THE INDIANS had left for their homes and the people of that province got news of what had taken place with us, they, being friends of the Christians, came to see us, bringing beads and feathers. We ordered them to build churches and put crosses in them, which until then they had not done. We also sent for the children of the chiefs to be baptized. Then the captain pledged himself before God not to make a raid or allow one to be made or to capture slaves from the people and in the country we had set at peace again. He promised to keep and fulfill this vow until His Majesty and the governor, Nuño de Guzman, or the viceroy, in his name, ordained something better adapted to the service of God and of His Majesty.

After baptizing the children we left for the village of San Miguel, where, on our arrival, Indians came and recounted how many people were coming down from the mountains, settling on the plain, building churches and erecting crosses; in short, complying with what we had sent them word to do. Day after day we were getting news of how all was being done and completed.

Fifteen days after our arrival Alcaraz came in with the Christians who had been on that raid and told the captain how the Indians had come down from the mountains and settled on the plain and that villages formerly deserted were now well populated, that the Indians had come out to welcome them with crosses in their hands, had taken them to their houses, had given them some of what they had, and how they had slept the night there. Amazed at these changes and at the words of the Indians who said they felt secure, he ordered that no harm be done to them, and with this they departed. May God in his infinite mercy grant that in the days of Your Majesty and under your power and sway, these people become willingly and sincerely subjects of the true Lord who created and redeemed them. We believe they will be, and that Your Majesty is destined to bring it about, because it will not be at all difficult.

In the two thousand leagues we traveled, on land, and by sea in boats, and in the ten months more after our rescue from captivity that we untiringly walked across the land, nowhere did we come upon either sacrifices or idolatry. During all that time we crossed from one ocean to the other, and from what we very carefully ascertained there may be, from one coast to the other and across the greatest width, two hundred leagues. We heard that on the shores of the south there are pearls and great wealth, and that the richest and best is near there.

We remained at the village of San Miguel until after the fifteenth of May, because from there to the town of Compostela—where the governor, Nuño de Guzman, resided—there are one hundred leagues of deserted country threatened by hostiles, and we had to take an escort along. Twenty horsemen went with us, accompanying us as many as forty leagues. Afterward we had with us six Christians, who escorted five hundred Indian captives. When we reached Compostela, the governor received us very well. He gave us what he had for us to wear, but for many days I could bear no clothing, nor could we sleep anywhere but on the bare floor. Ten or twelve days later we left for Mexico.[79] On the whole trip the Christians treated us well. Many came to see us on the road, praising God for having freed us from so many dangers. We reached Mexico on Sunday, the day before the vespers of Saint James, and were very well received by the Viceroy and the Marquis of the Valley,[80] who presented us with clothing, offering all they had. On the day of Saint James there was a festival, with bullfight and tournament.[81]

CHAPTER THIRTY-SEVEN

What Occurred When I Wished to Return

AFTER TAKING TWO MONTHS' REST AT MEXICO, I wished to come over to this realm. In October, when we were about to sail, a storm wrecked the ship and it was lost. With this in mind, I decided to wait until winter was over, since in these parts navigation is very dangerous then on account of storms.

When winter was past, Andrés Dorantes and I left Mexico, during Lent, for Vera Cruz, to take a ship there, but again had to wait for favorable winds until Palm Sunday. We embarked and were on board more than fifteen days, unable to leave on account of a calm. The ship began to fill with water so I left it and took passage on one of the ships that was in condition to leave. Dorantes remained on the first one, and on the tenth day of the month three craft left port.

We sailed together for 150 leagues. Afterward two of the ships took on water and dropped behind, and in the course of the night we lost track of them. It seems that, as we found out later, their pilots and skippers did not venture any further, and returned to port without giving us any warning; neither did we hear any more from them.[82] So we kept on, and on the fourth of May reached the port of Havana, on the Island of Cuba, where we waited until the second of June, still hoping for the other two vessels to arrive, when we left. We were afraid of falling in with French craft that only a few days before had captured three of ours.

In the vicinity of the island of Bermuda a storm overtook us, as is quite usual in those parts—according to the people who travel in them—and for a whole night we considered ourselves lost. But it pleased God that, when morning came, the storm abated and we were able to proceed on our way. Twenty-nine days after sailing from Havana we had made eleven hundred leagues, said to be the distance from it to the settlement of the Azores, and the next day we passed the island of Corvo,[83] and met with a French vessel at noon. She began to follow us, having with her a caravel taken from the Portuguese, and chased us. That same evening we saw nine more ships, but at such a distance that we could not distinguish whether they were of the same nation as our pursuer, or Portuguese. At nightfall the Frenchman was but a cannon shot from our ship and as soon as it was dark we changed our course in order to get away from him. Since he was close upon us he saw our maneuver and did the same, which happened three or four times.

The Frenchman could have taken us then, but he preferred to wait until daylight. It pleased God that, when morning came, we found ourselves, as well as the French ship, surrounded by the nine craft we had seen the evening before, and which turned out to belong to the Portuguese navy. I thank our Lord for having allowed me to escape from the tribulations of land and the perils of the sea.

When the French saw it was the Portuguese fleet they released the caravel, which was filled with Negroes. They had taken it along in order to make us believe they were Portuguese and to induce us to wait for them. On separating from the caravel the Frenchman told the skipper and the pilot we were French, too, and belonged to their own navy. They then put sixty oarsmen into their vessel, and thus, by oar and sail, went off with incredible swiftness.

The caravel then approached the galley warning its captain that both our vessel and the other were French, so that when we came up to the galley and the squadron with it, believing us to be French, they cleared for action and came to attack us. But when we were near enough to them we hailed them and they saw we were friends. They had been deceived, suffering the privateer's escape by means of his strategy of telling them that we were also French. Four caravels went in pursuit of him. We came up with the galley and presented our respects and the captain, Diego de Silveira, asked where we came from and what we had on board. We told him we were from New Spain, and that we carried silver and gold. He inquired how much it might be, and the skipper informed him that we had about three hundred thousand Castellanos.[84] Thereupon the captain exclaimed: "I'faith, you come back very rich, though you have a bad craft and miserable artillery. That whoreson dog of a French renegade has lost a fat morsel, God knows! Now that you have escaped; follow me closely, and God helping, I shall lead you back to Castile."[85]

The caravels that had gone in pursuit of the French soon returned because the latter sailed too fast for them and they did not want to leave their squadron, which was escorting three ships loaded with spices.

We reached the Island of Tercera,[86] where we rested fifteen days and took on supplies as well as waiting for another ship from India with the same kind of cargo as the three our fleet was escorting. At the end of the fifteen days we sailed together for the port of Lisbon, where we arrived on the ninth of August, vespers of Saint Laurentius day, of the year 1537.

And, in testimony of that what I have stated in the foregoing narrative is true, I hereunto sign my name:

Cabeza de Vaca

[The document from which this is taken was signed with his name and bore the seal with his coat of arms.]

CHAPTER THIRTY-EIGHT

What Happened to the Others Who Went to the Indies

SINCE, IN FOREGOING NARRATIVE, I have related the journey, the arrival at, and the departure from the country, and return to this realm, I now also wish to tell what happened to the ships and to the people who remained on board them. I have not yet said anything about them, for the reason that we heard nothing of their fate until after our return, when we found many of the survivors in New Spain and some here in Castile. Through them we learned everything that occurred after we had left the three ships, one having been lost previously on the wild coast.

The ships remained in great danger, since they had on board a hundred people and few supplies. Among them were ten married women, one of whom had foretold the governor many things that afterward happened to him.

When he marched inland she warned him not to go, saying that neither he nor any of his company would return, and that, should any come back, God would work miracles through him, since she felt sure that few, or none, would escape. The governor responded that he and all who went with him expected to fight and conquer many and very strange people and countries, so that, while many would have to die in the conquest, he was sure, from the accounts he had of the richness of the country, that the survivors would be fortunate and become very wealthy, according to the information about the riches that land contained. He asked the woman to tell him who it was that had acquainted her with the things, past and present, of which she had spoken. She answered that in Castile a Moorish woman from Hornachos had told her what she said to us before we left there, all of which took place as predicted.[87]

After the governor had appointed for his lieutenant and commander of all the vessels and their crews one Caravallo, a native of Cuenca de Huete,[88] we marched off, the governor leaving orders that they embark at once and proceed to Pánuco, always hugging the coast and keeping a lookout for the port where, when found, they should wait for us.

At the time the people were embarking, some saw, and distinctly overheard, the aforementioned woman saying to the other women that, since their husbands had gone inland to place themselves in such imminent danger, they should not think of them any longer, but at once look for other husbands; that she was going to do it, for her part. So she and the others married and lived with those that were on board the vessels.

The ships set sail and went on, but did not find any port in the direction they were proceeding, so they turned around and went back where, five leagues further down from our landing place, they came upon the harbor. It stretched inland for seven or eight leagues and was the one we had already discovered and where we had found the boxes from Spain, as we said earlier, where the bodies of Christians were. From this harbor and along that coast the three vessels, together with one that rejoined them from Havana and the brigantine, cruised in search of us for nearly a year, and then, not finding us, they went to New Spain.

That harbor is the best on earth. It sweeps inland for seven or eight leagues; the water is six fathoms deep at the mouth and five near the shore; the bottom is mud, and there are no tides inside the bay, or heavy storms. There is space in it for many ships, and it has many fish. The distance from it to Havana, a Christian town on Cuba, is one hundred leagues on a line from north to south. Its breezes are constant, and the trip is made from one place to the other in four days, because the vessels go and come with little trouble.

Now that I have given an account of the ships, it may be well to record also who it pleased God to rescue from all these dangers and hardships and where in this kingdom they are from. The first is Alonso del Castillo Maldonado, a native of Salamanca[89] and son of Doctor Castillo and Doña Aldonza Maldonado. The second is Andrés Dorantes, son of Pablo Dorantes, born at Béjar,[90] but a resident of Gibraléon.[91] The third is Alvar Núñez Cabeza de Vaca, son of

Francisco de Vera and grandson of Pedro de Vera, who conquered
the Canary Islands. His mother was called Doña Teresa Cabeza de
Vaca, and she was a native of Xerez de la Frontera. The fourth was
Estevanico, an Arab Negro from Azamor.[92]

End

COLOPHON

This treatise was printed in the magnificent, noble, and ancient city of Zamora by the honorable Agustín de Paz and Juan Picardo, partners in a printing firm and residents of the aforementioned city. The costs were underwritten by the virtuous Juan Pedro Musetti, book merchant and resident of Medina del Campo. It was completed on the sixth of October, the year of our Lord and Savior Jesus Christ, one thousand five hundred forty-two.

NOTES

1. The administrative capital of the Indies, Seville (Sevilla) was the starting point for many expeditions. Many of the voluminous records of the conquest of the Indies remain in Seville to this day, at the Archivo General de Indias (General Archive of the Indies).
2. The title given to Pánfilo de Narváez's was *adelantado*, and he is generally referred throughout as *governador*, or governor. See also note 10.
3. The Chronicle's prologue, or *Proema*, is a highly stylized introduction that begins with the traditional *laudatio* in praise of the monarch and continues with justifications for the work itself. In it Cabeza de Vaca begins the defense of his actions and reformulates his failure, making it into a useful endeavor. Bandelier does not include the prologue in her translation of the text.
4. In the 1555 edition, Cabeza de Vaca changes this to ten years, which is approximately the time he spent away from Spain. Nine years represents the period from the time he left Spain to the point at which he meets the Spaniards (chapter 33).
5. Dates are reckoned in the Julian calendar. For dates according to the Gregorian calendar, add ten days.
6. San Lúcar de Barrameda is located near the mouth of the Guadalquivir River in southern Spain. In the sixteenth century, it was the point of departure for many expeditions to the Indies.
7. The Emperor Charles V.
8. The modern-day Río de Soto la Marina in the State of Tamaulipas (Mexico).
9. The present-day Florida peninsula.
10. As the expedition's treasurer, Cabeza de Vaca was expected to give an accounting of all income and collect taxes for the crown. His claim to having been appointed to the position of chief legal officer (*alguacil mayor*) may be specious. According to Adorno and Pautz, not only is there no documentary evidence to support this appointment, but contrary evidence exists that this post was occupied by the expedition's leader, Narváez.
11. Like the treasurer, the comptroller, tax agent, and inspector are officials of the royal treasury.

12. In the opening to the 1542 edition, Cabeza de Vaca identifies the commissary as "Gutierrez." Later in the text, he will be called Xuarez (Suarez, in modern Spanish). In the 1555 edition, he is only identified as "Xuarez," which is consistent with administrative documents of the expedition.

13. The island of Hispañola, or Hispaniola, in the Caribbean Sea. The island is currently divided between the Spanish-speaking Dominican Republic on the east and the French-speaking Haiti on the west.

14. Santiago lies on the southeastern coast of the island of Cuba, in the northeastern Caribbean.

15. Vasco Porcallo de Figueroa was a major figure in the early Spanish development of Cuba. He also accompanied Hernando de Soto on his 1539 expedition on the North American mainland. For more information on Porcallo, see the chronicle of the de Soto expedition by the Gentleman of Elvas.

16. Trinidad lies on the south-central coast of Cuba.

17. A Spanish league varied between 2.7 and 3.1 miles, depending on the region of the country in which it was measured.

18. A spur of land on the southern coast of Cuba. The original Spanish reads "Cabo Cruz."

19. This is often thought to be the first European account of a hurricane.

20. It is unclear why it was requested that Cabeza de Vaca receive the supplies or who made the request. If it had been Porcallo or Pantoja, one would assume that Cabeza de Vaca would have identified him.

21. This refers to Spain, to which Cabeza de Vaca had already returned when he wrote this account.

22. The present-day port of Cienfuegos, on the south-central coast of Cuba.

23. Though the original reads "on the coast of Lixarte," in the 1555 edition, Cabeza de Vaca changed it to "the coast of Havana," and Bandelier follows suit.

24. The Canarroe shoals are an archipelago off the southern coast of Cuba.

25. A town in western Cuba (Pilar del Río Province).

26. A spur of land on the western edge of Cuba.

27. Again, a section on the western edge of Cuba.

28. Bandelier translates the Spanish *maíz* as "maize," except when the text refers to the meal made from *maíz*, which she translates as "cornmeal." Though the English word *maize* often brings with it connotations of Mesoamerica, and Adorno and Pautz make a case for the specific type of maize that probably migrated thousands of years ago from Mexico, I prefer the more commonly used English word.

29. The Spanish settlements of Central Mexico, in which the capital city lay.

30. The section of contemporary Florida that runs approximately from Tampa Bay to the Apalachicola River.

31. The Spanish settlements in the vicinity of the Pánuco River (Río Pánuco), on the northeastern coast of contemporary Mexico.

32. The central province of Spain, where the capital city of Madrid lies. From there, Ferdinand and Isabella conquered the remaining Moorish states and created the modern Spanish state.

33. The original text reads "alcalde."

34. The region of southern Spain in which Seville lies and from which the exploration embarked.

35. A city in Castile. Narváez himself is thought to have been a native of the area. In the original, the vague use of pronouns makes it unclear if the Spaniards went after the horse or the man, but the inference is that they went in search of Velázquez's body (though according to the text they retrieved the horse as well, and had him for dinner), so instead of a "him," for the sake of clarity, Velazquez's name is inserted.

36. June 25. The Feast of Saint John is June 24.

37. Adorno and Pautz identify this as "the island of Djerba, located off southeastern Tunisia in the Mediterranean at the entrance to Gabes." Others have suggested that it may be the town of Gelves in Andalusia (Spain).

38. This may be the first European sighting of the common opossum (Didelphis virginiana).

39. This is a puzzling statement, since if the Spanish landed in Florida a few days before Easter, it would have been midsummer when the Narváez party reached Apalache.

40. Tezaico in the original.

41. Aute was most likely located near the present-day site of St. Mark's, Florida.

42. Most likely this relates to the English span. According to the Oxford English Dictionary, a span is "the distance taken from the tip of the thumb to the tip of the little finger . . . when the hand is extended," or about nine inches.

43. Most likely one of the several rivers that empty into the Apalachee Bay.

44. The original Spanish is ambiguous, and both the original and Bandelier's translation lead the reader to conclude the opposite of Cabeza de Vaca's obvious intention. It has been modified in this translation.

45. The Spanish word for these vessels is *barca*, which Bandelier translates as "barge" and others have translated as "raft," though later descriptions and Cabeza de Vaca's earlier use of the word *balsa* for raft seem to preclude the latter. In Spain at that time, small boats called *barcas* were used for coastal fishing. These rudimentary craft may have approximated the size and appearance of these coastal craft.

46. A Spanish measurement of dry volume equivalent to about 1.5 bushels.
47. Spanish *codos*. Cubits represented various lengths. These were most likely about eighteen inches, and meant that the boats would have been about thirty-three feet long.
48. September 29.
49. This is generally thought to be Galveston Island.
50. A city in western Castile.
51. A city in the province of Badajoz, in southwestern Spain.
52. Omitted in the 1555 edition, the island remains unidentified.
53. Spanish, Isla de Malhado, literally, island of bad fate.
54. In the 1555 edition, this is changed to "cane weirs" (cane fishnets).
55. Spanish, *físicos*. Later in the text, Cabeza de Vaca will also refer to these men (and himself) as *médicos*. Bandelier translated both words as "medicine men," and though this brings with it the connotation of primitivism, this does appear to be Cabeza de Vaca's intent.
56. Some translations have concluded that "Asturiano" was the priest's name.
57. At this point Bandelier adds from the 1555 edition, "This Indian, his wife, their son and another Indian who was with them were all cross-eyed." The original reads *tuerto*, which can mean cross-eyed, one-eyed, or blind in one eye and most recent translators have opted for the last. See introduction for additional information.
58. Though the spelling of the names of Indian nations in Cabeza de Vaca varies, they have been made consistent for this translation. For more information on the Indian nations Cabeza de Vaca encountered, see Pupo-Walker's edition of *Castaways*.
59. The original reads *arcos*, which can be translated as either "bows" or the more architectural "arches."
60. Bandelier translates this as leprosy, which may have been Cabeza de Vaca's intent. The Lazarus to whom he refers appears in the Gospel according to Saint Luke 16:20–21. "And then there was a certain beggar named Lazarus, which was laid at his gate, full of sores. And desiring to be fed with crumbs which fell from the rich man's table; moreover the dogs came and licked his sores" (King James Version).
61. Although Cabeza de Vaca calls these animals "cows" (*vacas*), judging from the description of their physical attributes and their migrations, it is probable that he is describing the American bison, or buffalo.
62. Cabeza de Vaca's own early military training took place in the wars in Italy (see introduction).
63. This list of Indian nations reflects Cabeza de Vaca's temporal and spatial viewpoint. His characterization of Indians as "recent" reflects the point in time he has reached in his travel narrative. Instead of the direc-

tions of north, south, east, and west, he situates tribes in relation to each other and local landmarks. Bandelier is highly skeptical of the reliability of the names of these tribes and does not believe that Cabeza de Vaca had very much understanding of the tribal names or locations.

64. A liquid measure that is reckoned by weight, generally about twenty-five pounds, more or less between two and four gallons.

65. The Guadalquivir.

66. Bandelier points out that these dances generally comprised a religious ceremony and not "mere rejoicing," which, she believes, Cabeza de Vaca "of course, did not, and could not, know."

67. Most scholars believe that this refers to the Gulf of Mexico. When Cabeza de Vaca talks of the South Sea, he is generally referring to the Gulf of California.

68. Bandelier points out that in the 1555 edition, Cabeza de Vaca changed this to "margarita," and believes it was mica.

69. Bandelier identifies this as Pinnus edulis.

70. Bandelier adds the following from the 1555 edition: "The cut I had made only showed a scar like a line in the palm of the hand." In the second edition of h:s account, Cabeza de Vaca wanted to show himself as a superior doctor, which may be evidence of an important aspect of his objective in composing that edition.

71. Bandelier states that "this recalls the ceremonial rabbit-hunt of the Pueblo Indians of New Mexico."

72. According to Bandelier, the "village of the 'hearts' is a point well established in southern central Sonora. (See "The Journey of Coronado," in this series, by Mr. Winship.)" Bandelier refers to the A.S. Barnes publication by George Parker Winship.

73. Cabeza de Vaca implies that, if the Spanish had come there only for the purpose of discovering or exploring new territories, and not for settlement, they might not return to the region at all and the four would have to continue to wander.

74. According to Bandelier, this is the Petatlan River.

75. The Spanish colonial province to the west of New Spain, along the coast of the Gulf of California.

76. Bandelier notes that "(i)t is not unlikely that they were malachites. I saw, in possession of a prominent medicine-man from the Pueblo of San Juan, in New Mexico, a plate of malachite shaped like a large, blunt knife, which he said had come from Chihuahua. It was, of course, not transparent, but had a fine emerald hue. In South America (Peru and Bolivia) among the common people emeralds having a so-called 'garden'—that is, imperfectly transparent specimens—are highly prized, provided their color is deep green."

77. Primahaitu may have been Cabeza de Vaca's transcription of the name of the language spoken by the Pima Indians, who inhabited the region around Culiacán. Bizcaya is the Basque region of northern Spain. Bandelier suggests that because Cabeza de Vaca may have found Primahaitu very difficult to learn or understand, as is Euskadi for non-Basques, for that reason Cabeza de Vaca made reference to it here, and related the two.

78. Bandelier adds in a note, "For Melchor Diaz and his career, see 'The Journey of Coronado.' He was entirely different from Alcaraz and Cebreros, and of uncommon ability and energy, while at the same time cautious and humane."

79. In English, this is known as Mexico City.

80. Hernán de Cortés (1485–1547). In an ironic twist, in the early 1520s, Cortés had imprisoned Pánphilo de Narváez, who, it appears, was intriguing for power in Mexico (see introduction). Cortés must have taken great pleasure in hearing of Narváez's ignominy and death.

81. The original reads *juego de cañas*, a militaristic sport with some aspects of jousting.

82. According to Bandelier's note, "This explains why Dorantes remained in Mexico, where he afterward attempted to set on foot an expedition to the north, but failed."

83. Corvo is a member of the Azores group of islands.

84. Castellanos were a unit of currency equal to one-fiftieth of a gold mark.

85. Following is the original speech, in the argot of the Portuguese naval captain, as reported by Cabeza de Vaca and broken down into readable sentences: "Boase, que venís muito ricos, pero trazedes muy ruin navío y muyto ruyn artilleria. O, fi de puta caun arrenegado françes, que bon bocado, per de bota Deus. Ora sus poys vos avedes escapado seguime. Non vos apartades de mí que con ayuda de Deus eu vos porne en Castela."

86. Tercera (Terceira) is a member of the Azores group of islands, east-southeast of Corvo (see note 83).

87. There have been many interpretations of this passage and why Cabeza de Vaca included it. He may have wanted to provide further evidence of Pánfilo de Narváez's incompetence, especially if he felt that his audience might have believed such predictions where Narváez did not. Whether the prediction took place at all is also a matter of controversy.

88. Huete is a town in the province of Cuenca, east-southeast of Madrid.

89. A university and cathedral city west-northwest of Madrid.

90. Bejar del Castenar, a town west of Madrid.

91. Gibraleon, in the province of Huelva, in southwestern Spain.

92. Azamor, or Azemmour, is a city on the western coast of Morocco. It is

thought that Estevanico was enslaved there when the Portuguese conquered the city in 1513, and then sold to Andrés Dorantes. Estevanico
later led an expedition from Mexico City back to the north, in the
party of Fray Marcos de Niza, the chronicle of which Bandelier includes as the second part of her book on Cabeza de Vaca.